PREVAIL

A comprehensive summary of leadership disciplines that will make you ready for what's next

ABDULAZIZ AL-ROOMI

PASSIONPRENEUR®
PUBLISHING

Publishing information
Publishing, design, and production facilitated by Passionpreneur Publishing, A division of Passionpreneur Organization Pty Ltd, ABN: 48640637529

www.PassionpreneurPublishing.com
Melbourne, VIC | Australia

DEDICATION

I dedicate this book to:

My late grandmother, Shaikha Al-Zahim, and late grandfather, Ali Al-Roomi, as a continuation of their publishing journey.

My mother for her keen focus on my education and for always pushing me to be the best at whatever I do.

My father for setting a living example of an authentic, genuine, and caring leader.

My wife for believing in me and doing her best to help me in writing my book and achieving my personal vision.

All my leaders, managers and colleagues who helped me through my career and enriched my understanding of good leadership practices; I have used their personal actions and stories as examples in my book.

CONTENTS

Dedication   iii
Foreword   vii
Personal Reflections   xi
Introduction   xix

CHAPTER 1: The Effective Leadership System   1

CHAPTER 2: A Leading Self Creates Great Leaders   13
Nature or Nurture?   17
Personal Mastery   29

CHAPTER 3: Formula of Influence   41
Score Credibility   45
Be an Authority   61
Communicate with Impact   75
Add Value to Others   91

CHAPTER 4: As in Times of War   103
Build Your Team of Warriors   107
Warriors Assemble   125
Choose Your Battles   141

CHAPTER 5: Pull the Trigger   153
Where to Start?   157
Team of Unstoppables   175

CHAPTER 6: The Prevail Leadership Model   189

Conclusion   201
Whistles of Acknowledgment   205

FOREWORD

BY MARSHALL GOLDSMITH

The moment I picked up Prevail, I immediately knew I had something special in my hands. Prevail is an exceptional leadership manual. It creates a roadmap for aspiring leaders to grow their careers by developing an authentic leadership brand to help them become successful at any given time and in any environment.

As the leading expert in the field of Behavioral Change and Executive Coaching, I have over four decades of experience helping top CEOs and executives achieve lasting, positive change in their leadership. Through working with these incredible people, I've found that it takes something truly different to stand out from the noise in a field so saturated with conventional wisdom. Prevail is the guide to getting that unique factor.

When I met Abdulaziz (Aziz) in 2012 in Kuwait, I was impressed by his passion for developing people in the leadership field. It's clear that since then, Aziz has been enriching his experience and sharpening his skills as a leadership coach, trainer, and thought leader. With hands-on experience, exposure to global best practices, continuous learning and a mindset to help others help themselves, Aziz is quickly becoming one of the best coaching thought leaders.

What is so unique about Prevail is that it's about realizing human potential through the lens of being an authentic leader. It's a fresh take on how to overcome challenges while being true to yourself and others — a bold approach that comes from characteristics of humility and genuine care for those you lead. The direct style of the book is one of its strengths, and the vast range of stories and examples that it contains makes it a truly global reference across cultures and positions.

The Prevail Leadership Model makes Aziz's principles simple by combining well-known, proven techniques into a practical model that will help leaders and high-potentials become more impactful and effective in their behavior, leadership, and ability to deliver results.

My mission is simple. I want to help successful people achieve positive, lasting change in behavior - for themselves, their people, and their teams. I don't do this for fame and accolades. I do this because I love helping people! Aziz shares the same passion and mission; that is clear in this book. Read it and follow his advice!

Marshall Goldsmith
Thinkers50 #1 Executive Coach and New York Times
bestselling author of What Got You Here Won't Get You
There, Triggers and Mojo.

BOOK TESTIMONY BY JACK ZENGER

"This book is a wonderful compilation of the best thinking about the broad topic of leadership development from one of the most insightful thought leaders of the past seven decades. This information is brought together in a cohesive way and it will become a useful template for anyone aspiring to become a better leader. Highly recommended!"

Jack Zenger, CEO of Zenger Folkman,
co-author of the best-selling
The New Extraordinary Leader:
Turning Good Managers into Great Leaders.

PERSONAL REFLECTIONS

In my career, I have worked in multiple departments, moving from IT to HR to leadership training and development. My work involved impacting and influencing professional clients and colleagues, leading teams and organizations, and changing initiatives and activities. Throughout the way, I noted different challenges that every leader-to-be needs to manage while prevailing and helping others. Developing the right know-how to lead effectively and efficiently requires an individual, consistent effort and the presence of the right mentor (or coach). Without someone to observe you and give you feedback, it's very difficult to assess your performance. Even if you are confident that you're doing well, you can still be wrong because you're limited to seeing things from your own perspective. This is a struggle I have constantly witnessed in the field of leadership and employee development.

I have worked with leaders for the past sixteen years on performance management, leadership development programs, succession planning, employee development, coaching, change initiatives, training sessions, and so on. My focus has been on using a variety of different approaches, methods, and activities to improve execution, management and leadership behaviors.

Now I'm sharing the results of my journey.

Most leaders do not change. They might act a certain way for the sake of appearances, but they tend not to improve significantly or acquire new habits.

I have been involved in different management initiatives and leadership development activities, but people remain the same. Sometimes, they maneuver in various ways or they act like they have changed; sometimes, they simply try to go around the system. Occasionally, they improve a bit for a while. But they always end up reverting to their original characters, flaws and weaknesses, and deficient leadership behaviors.

Leaders and managers can be the worst when it comes to accountability. In my experience, because they are influential, they can get away with a lot. Consequently, you need to provide them with different solutions, which calls for a lot of investment, especially when it comes to leadership training; the higher the rank, the more the investment required and the more the cost will be. Sometimes, a leader's development cost is equal to or even more than the development cost of ten employees. In other words, the 10% of employees who are leaders, managers, and senior managers receive an equal amount of investment in terms of money compared to the rest of the employees; it is weird because leaders are expected to improve, and, yet, are surprisingly resistant to change.

Decisions made by leaders and managers significantly impact the organization, yet, as I said, they face few, if any, consequences for poor decisions or mismanagement. In my experience, it's quite rare to see leaders who really take the time and effort to improve. There are many reasons for this.

First of all, from a management's perspective, leadership development initiatives are a secondary concern, not a primary one. The primary one, of course, is making money. This is understandable, but it means that any effort to improve leadership that isn't directly focused on maximizing revenue is going to be sidelined or ignored.

The second issue is that leaders don't always see improvement as something tangible. They live in a work environment governed by metrics—quarterly profit reports, sales, and all the data that corporations spend time and money gathering. They'd rather spend more time on the tangible, measurable activities and performance indicators than on something as abstract as leadership skills. Leadership is considered to be a soft skill and more of an intangible or subjective development matter. It can be observed, but the return on the bottom line is not directly visible.

The other thing is that usually, people in power simply don't want to change. They have worked hard to achieve their status, and they are too secure in their positions. They do not feel threatened by consequences for failing to change the way they behave, and changing behavior is very difficult at all levels to begin with. The older you are or the more important your job title, the tougher it is for you to be convinced that you need to improve. "Why do I need to improve if I'm already doing well?"

Those are the main challenges I faced in working to improve the behavior of employees, leaders, and managers. However, a few people did actually redefine themselves and continued to work on upgrading their skills and characters. What makes these leaders different is that they are resilient and have a mindset that allows for growth. They are, dedicated to improving their personalities and characters—basically, their aspirations and ambitions. Usually, they want to be more affluent and more successful—someone who is among the most respected of leaders. The majority, however, don't care. They blame their failures on politics, culture, or somebody else. However, the few who change and are recognized by the organization as change agents are mostly the top leaders. They show significant change and are really keen on taking any opportunity for development, as long as it is well-regarded and they see the value of the initiative.

THE "AHA" MOMENT

To make any headway, you need to get their buy-in! In order to have an effective process to become successful or to have more effective leadership, we need to have a system that holds its leaders accountable. It needs to be clear, practical, and applicable to all types of leadership situations and teams. In order to overcome the challenges, the leaders who are engaged in the solutions need to feel that they can apply the techniques to their work. They should be assured that the techniques are relevant to them, are simple, and can be understood and observed. Leaders want to be recognized for their newly acquired positive behavior. So, we need to consider this when coming up with any solution. At the end of my learning and development journey, this is how I was able to successfully gain buy-in from leaders.

To be an impactful, inspiring, and memorable leader who is well-placed to move up the ladder, you need to acknowledge your strengths and what you like to do in order to be able to go the extra mile and prevail over the rest.

Although it might seem frustrating, when you see people improve and admire your follow-up, work, and support, then it is all worth the effort and the struggles. According to the 10/20/70* Model, improvement involves 10% training, 20% coaching, and 70% learning on the job. Most leaders and individuals spend a lot of their money on the training part. Organizations also invest in training, and will send personnel to top schools for executive training, and so on and so forth. Though expensive, it only counts as 10% of the overall journey. But people are very keen on such schemes; they like to drop names of prestigious institutions and programs, mentioning that they have attended training at Harvard or MIT for example. However, a fancy institutional pedigree doesn't mean that they really have improved or gained any skills. Even as enablers of training and development, we need to consider this while we are developing and designing training programs. This is important for Learning & Development and HR departments. From my global experience in the practices necessary to change behavior in the workplace, I can say that it takes six to twenty-four months to effectively incorporate new activities or approaches into your new leadership style. So, it takes no less than six months and no more than twenty-four months for a person to learn and apply the mentioned model in order to fully acquire and adapt to the new style. The person then moves from point A to point B; this applies to leaders and non-leaders as well. This has been my experience in training leaders since 2011.

So, in order to keep focus and accomplish the above model, we need to have some type of an easy, clear, simple tool and method to follow up throughout the way. What I have realized is that leadership is everyone's job, and it's a nonstop journey. Everyone has a chance every day to prove to themselves and to others that they are leaders. If you are a leader, then you are under the microscope; you're being observed and are considered to be a role model. Leaders are considered to be like parents; that's what I keep telling my clients and the people I work with. If they are tough, then they do it for the benefit of their team members and the organization. They need to have that extra vision for the individuals and the company while they are coaching, giving feedback, or giving an assignment to help the team to grow in its character or performance.

That's a powerful role, and you need to live up to it. You need to learn to walk before you can run. Leadership is challenging. It's a different ball game from being a personal contributor; there are many more elements that affect you as a leader. However, you need to take it step by step. There is a solution and a way, if you are willing to take that way and be perceived as a leader—both by your team and by others.

WHY AM I WRITING A BOOK?

When I envision my legacy, I want to be remembered as a person who created value. I'm a person who adds value to the world by helping others realize their contributions to society through personal development. How do I do that? By helping others realize their values and potential. This is a general philosophy that I pursue both in my own life and when interacting with others. However, my job is to help leaders become better—because better leaders create a better world, a better society, and a better environment, whether in a corporate or non-corporate environment, and, eventually, a better future for all! Nevertheless, my focus is on the organizational environment, which is where I have the most expertise. My personal vision and values align with helping people develop their own genuine, authentic leadership model. So, that's why I do it, and that's why I care about it.

INTRODUCTION

D o you want to live a mindful life and be content with yourself? How important is it for you to visualize your dreams and achieve them?

How much do you want to be popular and credible, to feel valued by peers and colleagues?

How important is it for you to be an inspiring leader, be known as a winner, and be perceived as genuine?

Imagine yourself having all these qualities. It's possible, just by spending an hour or two reading this book and practicing some of the techniques inside—well-known practices that have proven to be successful, and tools that have impacted and positively changed millions of lives, including mine!

It's all here, right within your hands!

Are you looking for a path to greatness, your greatness? Whether your answer is "yes" or "not yet," this book can be your guide to achieving success!

Many people ask themselves, "Why should I lead others? Why become responsible for other people and be blamed for other people's mistakes?" Leaders are often the first to be held responsible for problems and the last to get the credit for success! Yet, for many, especially in the Middle East and North Africa regions, people seek leadership positions in pursuit of higher salaries and social status. Unfortunately, without the right mindset, tools, and preparation, they soon realize it can be a nightmare! Most leaders are not the happiest people, nor the most popular in the workplace. What can we do about it? How many popular leaders do you remember, compared to the bad ones?

This book provides you with a simple way to practice the essentials of effective leadership. In these pages, you'll learn how to use these tools to your advantage and achieve your personal and career goals.

There are many powerful and well-known leadership theories that I have combined in a visual model to help leaders realize and capitalize on their strengths. This will help you create a positive impact on your organization and other people. I hope it will also make you interested in learning more.

This book will help you find your true north in your leadership compass. You'll be remembered as a solid leader who can take his or her team to the next level of the game!

It provides a holistic approach to the principles of effective leadership that will differentiate you from the rest if you apply it to your life.

The main lessons of Prevail focus on how to lead your life according to your values, acknowledge your strengths, and influence the right people to build positive collaborative relationships. This will enable you to motivate engaged teams to deliver exceptional results, and build your legacy.

You will learn how to reach your personal mastery, which is the cornerstone to help you understand how to achieve your personal vision, both in your career and your life; build a strong reputation that helps you gain supporters who care about you and want to help you to fulfill your goals and objectives; and learn what it requires to lead your team successfully and to continuously deliver results and meet stakeholders' expectations, which eventually will help you prevail as a leader who is ready for higher, more challenging roles.

The book provides guidelines, tools, and tips through a comprehensive development system to help current and future leaders succeed in their day-to-day leadership practices and projects. It contains global best practices and describes personal observations and experiences related to being an impactful leader.

I only preach what I have experienced and practiced. All the tools provided have helped me personally in my life and daily practices.

This book is not about life coaching or happiness, although happiness is a by-product of becoming an authentic person and leader. It provides a holistic approach that can be applied to your personal life and purpose and also world-class, simple techniques that can enhance your current and future leadership practices.

This isn't a reference book. This book is designed to help you become someone exceptional—someone known for the quality of their work, and a person who leaves an impact on their organization and those around them.

This leads us to Chapter 1, which explains the topics covered and the main takeaways you can expect to gain from this book.

Let's start the journey and prevail!

SOURCE

10/20/70* model: /https://trainingindustry.com/wiki/content-development/the-702010-model-for-learning-and-development/

CHAPTER 1

THE EFFECTIVE LEADERSHIP SYSTEM

Prevail: "Prove more powerful or superior; persuade (someone) to do something."

—Oxford Languages

PREFACE

In this chapter, we will talk about the four pillars of effective leadership: leading self, influencing others, leading teams, and motivation.

I selected these four pillars based on my personal experience and field practice in addition to the leadership theories from books such as Leadership and Motivation by John Adair, One Minute Manager by Ken Blanchard, How to Win Friends and Influence People by Dale Carnegie, and The Seven Habits of Highly Successful People by Stephen Covey, as well as well known thought leaders and various forms of leadership development and trainings that I have witnessed. So, what are the benefits that can be gained from reading this book? How will this book provide solutions for people who would like to be successful in their careers and lead teams? What should they expect while going through the book?

WHY?

People ask me for directions on how to lead, and my first thought is always to find the most effective and concise way to describe leadership. This is challenging because a lot of people have not been taught to take accountability or responsibility in their youth. In addition, these attitudes are reinforced by a strong cultural and intellectual style of living, which prevents us from being seen as independent people. This is reflected in our careers when we work in organizations or as entrepreneurs. People usually don't receive traditional or official leadership training and development until their late twenties or early thirties. Actually, they need it much earlier in their lives. The lucky ones realize the importance of leadership and influence early and they practice it on their own, whether this is in an NGO or college environment or simply during social engagements.

Lack of training, especially in the leadership area, is usually prevalent in the private and public sectors. When people look for solutions, they go for training, but this is only 10% of the development process. Truly effective development of leadership skills includes coaching and on-the-job practice as well. In the 10/20/70 Model, 10% is training, 20% is coaching, and 70% is on-the-job learning. I've provided advice and support to many leaders during my career in the area of leadership coaching and training. Usually, the information that we have is related to leadership assessments, performance evaluations, personality tests, 360-degree feedback, and interviews. This sort of information gives us a snapshot of the leader and a clue about what the weaknesses and strengths are in their behavioral leadership, but it doesn't show the root causes of these traits.

When we work with a leader to improve a weakness, we are fixing the problem for now, but that generally doesn't improve their overall leadership capability. On average, out of every five people who go through this kind of training, only one really shows major improvement and manages to sustain the improved or newly developed leadership skill for any length of time. Why does this happen? Basically, because old habits die hard. Everybody often goes back to the normal old mentality once the intervention of leadership development is complete. Especially in times of crisis, people tend to go back to their original habits. So, if they are hot-tempered, then they will revert to this pattern of behavior again. If they don't like to work in teams, they usually micromanage, so they will go back to micromanagement, and so on and so forth.

How can we provide you (as a leader), and everybody who's seeking assistance, with a way to maintain that improved behavior and continue to build even better behaviors?

When people undergo professional development and then return to their old behaviors, they lose credibility in front of the people around them. So, in order to deal with this, we need to build a measure of accountability into that person's developmental process. Why? In my experience, leadership development is usually conducted at the direction of an organization that pushes its leaders to improve. These leaders undergo the training out of obligation, rather than actually embracing it; in this circumstance, they're unlikely to change their mindset and learn to be more effective leaders.

In order to craft a solution that can tap into the mindset and get the buy-in from the leader in order to improve their leadership capabilities and sustain that improvement, I came up with this book to provide an approach that starts from the leader leading himself or herself and extends all the way to leading others. People, when they're in a leadership position, take a course and then management expects them to lead effectively. This is like asking people to run before they can walk. From my observations of leaders and managers in the many organizations I've been exposed to or worked with, it's common for leaders to deceive, manipulate, and hide behind others, sometimes taking the credit for work completed by their teams! These are clear examples of poor leadership and how leaders can fail to provide inspiration to others. Why do they do it? Because all they care about is the promotion, and are maybe satisfying a short-term goal and trying to do a quick fix on themselves and the team, hoping things will turn out for the best. Later on, they fall back into these bad behaviors. This is a common reason why talented people join companies only to leave shortly thereafter: poor leadership or poor management! We need to do something different and provide the leaders with solutions to continue being successful in spite of the challenges they face in leading others.

Part of my personal vision is to help people develop their own genuine, authentic leadership style. That is why I will spend most of this book building and enhancing the knowledge and skills you need to lead yourself and influence others before you can jump into leading teams effectively.

HOW?

In the next chapter, we will talk about the first element, leading self, which is divided into two main areas. First of all, I will help you understand the difference between leaders who are born and those who are made, the importance of having a personal vision and taking responsibility for your life, and how to live an intentional life.

The next section of leading self will examine personal mastery. What do you need in order to manage yourself effectively, and how do you get the right tools to lead yourself to achieve your vision?

With this, we conclude the discussion of tools, mindset, and theories regarding personal mastery and leading self. Then we'll talk about how to influence others in Chapter 3. This chapter is also divided into four main areas: (i) How to earn credibility by understanding the qualities that others admire in you; (ii) How to be an authority and a charismatic leader to build your personal brand; (iii) How to communicate with impact; and (iv) How to leave your mark.

With chapter 3, we wrap up the section on leading self and how to lead and win over others, your way.

Chapter 4 will cover how to build a winning team that delivers exceptional results. We will talk about optimal team structures, the requirements for building a winning team, and how to engage the team and make sure that they work with cohesiveness and the tools required to assign roles, set targets, and achieve them. This chapter will discuss all the elements of leading an effective team.

Then in Chapter 5, we'll cover a very essential element: motivation. We'll look at how it works and how you can motivate your team members.

In the last chapter, we will talk about The Leadership Triangles and The Prevail Leadership Model, recapping the highlights and building a model to help you put the approach into action.

LESSONS LEARNED

We talked about the first pillar, which is leading self, because if you don't know how to lead yourself, you will fail in leading others. If you don't know where you're going, you can't expect others to tell you.

The second pillar, influencing others, covers four important elements: credibility, charisma, know-how, and how to build productive relationships to help you achieve your vision.

The third pillar is how to lead your team to achieve exceptional results.

The fourth pillar is how to keep yourself and your team motivated. At the end, I will introduce The Prevail Leadership Model and The Leadership Triangle.

This will be your true north to move to the next level.

Let's start building, assessing, and consolidating your life vision, and learn how to embark on the journey of your personal greatness!

CHAPTER 2

A LEADING SELF CREATES GREAT LEADERS

"A genuine leader is not a searcher for consensus but a molder of consensus."

—Martin Luther King

NATURE OR NURTURE?

PREFACE

Who was your first leadership role model, inspiration, or mentor? What made them special? Can you be as inspiring as them? In order to successfully lead or influence others, you need to be perceived as a leader others want to follow! Leaders see the way, show the way, and lead the way; without a vision, there is no leadership. So, in order to lead ourselves and others, we need to have a vision of our own! The question is, where to start?

INTRODUCTION

In this chapter, we will dig deep into what you need to have to start an inspiring leadership journey. We will tap into what makes the right mindset while going through the current and future challenges and obstacles of your leadership story. Every true leader needs to lead themselves before they can effectively lead others. This requires them to be accountable for their life decisions and realize what they need to do to reach their dreams and career aspirations.

We will also explore how to pave the way to achieve our new purposeful intentional life, what we need in order to reach our goals, and how to overcome challenges while remaining focused on the end result.

WHY?

Are leaders born or made? By nature or by nurture?

It can be a long argument, but evidence has shown that leaders can, in fact, be made! In my opinion, every person is a potential leader at some point in time, whether by situational authority (parent, manager, etc.) or by choice (in NGOs, leading projects, socially, or politically).

Just to give you an idea of why leaders can be made and how leadership skills can be developed, I would encourage you to go to the top business schools' executive education pages and check their long list of Leadership Executive Development programs. Another example is Executive Leadership coaching, in which companies invest enormous amounts for their senior executives and future leaders. In a seminar, Tony Robbins' associate mentioned that Tony Robbins is paid more than a million dollars a year per executive for his coaching sessions! So, coaching sessions for a CEO—what does that say? It basically says that even if you are successful now, you need to work on improving your leadership skills because the world is changing, and there is always room to grow.

Whether you agree or are still skeptical about how successful "made" leaders are, let me tell you that I personally used to be a true believer in the idea that good leaders are born and not made. From what I experienced throughout my career, working closely with leaders (at work and in my personal life), it now seems to me that it all depends on the situation. A person can show the leadership qualities they have within them when their personal values or loved ones are intact. But the question is, how effective will your leadership capabilities be when you need them?

This question can be answered if you know what you want to achieve in your life and career and how to achieve it. All the most successful leaders made it because they were determined and continued to pursue their dreams and visions. Elon Musk, for example, is changing the world and changing the lives of people while he continues to take risks, despite that fact that he became filthy rich a long time ago. So why he is doing this?

HOW?

I will explain the first step of living a purposeful life, a life with meaning that ends with a legacy of your own.

The first step is to Take Responsibility for your life, decisions, and results, and stop blaming your parents, friends, society, or your cat. I realized the importance of this while watching one of Tony Robbins' videos where he explained it in a crystal clear way: be responsible for your life and admit failure! Once we acknowledge the importance of this, then we can accept the fact that we need to plan our lives to succeed in achieving our dreams and aspirations.

Before that—how to be sure that we have the right dream? Should it be money, fame, and other tangible materialistic goals, or it should be something else?

Going back to the question raised about your leadership role model: were they unique only because of their results? Let us take Muhammad Ali, for example, the greatest boxer of all time; do we revere him for what he achieved or how he achieved it? Let's take another example: Steve Jobs. He created Apple, a company that continued his legacy even after he died—the first company to earn a trillion dollars! Indeed, it was their unique drive, creativity, and determination that helped Jobs and Ali impact the other seven billion people on this planet. So what do we mean by the "How?" In Learning and Development and Talent Management, we refer to the answer to this question as behaviors. Behaviors reflect beliefs, and beliefs come from our values! Our actions, communication styles, and decisions are just the tip of the iceberg.

So what are values? Values are virtues and things that we cherish and admire; they drive us and excite us. They're what make us unique as individuals; we live our lives according to our values. A value can be based on family, teamwork, success, competence, competitiveness, trust, or any number of things. So a person will think, act, and perceive things from their value system. For example, Cristiano Ronaldo, the Portuguese football player, can be seen as someone who represents a competitive value because he's driven by competition. Steve Jobs was driven by innovation; Ali was also competitive and fair. So you cannot expect a person who embraces innovation or creativity as a value to be organized and conservative, and vice versa.

That was a brief about values and their impact on our lives. Now, in order to plan our lives around our values to live our dream lives in the way we want, we need to have our personal vision statement. In our Dale Carnegie training programs, we emphasize and practice writing and presenting personal vision statements. Vision statements can cover a time period of three months to three years or more into the future; it all depends on your specific vision. A personal vision might include a desired state at a specific point in time, such as losing five kilos in three months or attaining a Project Management Professional (PMP) certificate within six months. This is one part of the vision statement. Once you've identified the deliverables and time, then you need to express them using the following characteristics: present tense, powerful, and positive. You also need to include your personal feelings at that moment in time. Let's refer to the PMP example: "In six months' time, I will be hanging my PMP certificate in the middle of my office, feeling happy and proud and ready to take on my new project as PMP-certified." This positive and present-tense image will help you reenergize yourself to continue to pursue your career and life milestones when you feel down or like giving up.

A life vision statement should include your lifestyle and the way you want to live your life through your values. Let us take this example: "Living an adventurous joyful life by travel-ing around the world and meeting new people and making money out of it." So the values here are "joy," "adventure," and "lifestyle." You can have a career vision statement as well, which needs to be more structured around the follow-ing factors: your role, sector/industry, what you are good at, your values, and career aspirations. An example: "Being the CEO of a local bank, and being driven by my dedication and teamwork to provide help to less fortunate members of society." So you can see that dedication and teamwork are values, as is helping others.

As you see, the more we have a clear picture or aware-ness of what we want in our lives and careers, the better we enjoy them by achieving our milestones. Now, since all is clear at this point, we need to plan our life accordingly to achieve our vision. We need to start by "end in mind," so clearly identify the end results, and then break the journey down to short steps that can be achieved from today onward.

Now that we have a clear idea of what we want to achieve in the next few years and how to achieve it, we need to make sure that we do so with the right balance in our lives. In order to more easily do this, we can refer to the Wheel of Life, a globally recognized practical tool that gives you the current state of your life's dimensions on a scale of ten. It helps you to identify those parts of your life that you may be neglecting (intentionally or unintentionally), which is usually important to give us the right balance of work and life necessary to continue our personal and daily journey from a mindful perspective. The terms are general; for example, "financial" basically means how satisfied you are with your financial status. It has no relation to how much money you are making.

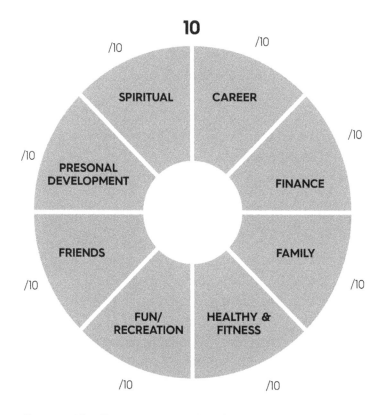

Resource: https://www.coachingwithnlp.co/coaching-wheel/

CONDITIONS FOR SUCCESS

If you are still hesitant to take action, take the time to answer the following questions.

- What if you don't have clear vision?
- What if you don't know your values?
- What if you don't plan your life and follow through?
- What if you don't take control of your life?

If you cannot come up with clear replies, the following considerations might clarify things for you.

Without vision, there will be nowhere to reach, nowhere to rest. That means you do not know what you want from life, what you want to be remembered for, and you're willing to be a victim of external conditions; basically, you're giving up on your dreams!

If you don't know your values, then you will not know what is important to you and what is the most important. You will lack in priorities in life and you will not be as great as you wish to be because you will be continuously changing to fulfill someone else's vision.

What if you aren't serious in planning your life? Then you will lose track because there is nothing against which to measure or compare your progress, unless you want to compare yourself with others—and that is the worst thing you can do! You will feel frustrated and most probably lose confidence in yourself.

What if you don't take control of your life? Someone else will!

LESSONS LEARNED

In this chapter, we have explored what you need to have in order to start an aspiring and intentional life.

We have covered how the right mindset to lead your life hinges on being responsible for your actions. If you want to be perceived as a leader and want others to follow you, then you need to show that you are an accountable person who takes care of your life before taking on the responsibility for the lives and actions of others. Then you can define your personal vision, and write your own vision statement, which includes your values. As per Ken Blanchard, a renowned authority in leadership, vision is important because personal vision reflects: "Who you are, where you want to be, and how to do it, and what will guide your journey." Well said, Ken! Here, we can see the sweet balance of vision and values that will help you reach your goals in life.

We concluded this chapter by discussing the importance of keeping things in perspective, identifying short- and long-term goals, and celebrating along the way—because you give yourself credit even if no one else does.

Last but not least, we introduced the Wheel of Life to help you balance your life as a human being so you are aware of the sacrifices you're willing to make along the way to live happily ever after!

CALL FOR ACTION

Write down your personal and career vision, according to your values.

Plan your life using the wheel of life.

Wheel of Life. Complete the Wheel of Life self-evaluation, then address the following:
- What you need to fix now (this will help you to have the right balance now).
- What you need to improve to achieve your personal vision (to keep moving).
- What you need to take care of while achieving your milestones (not to lose balance in the future).

> "You must expect great things of yourself before you can do them."
>
> —Michael Jordan

We have realized that we are all leaders and responsible professionals willing to take responsibility for our careers based on our vision and values, and that we plan our lives according to our standards. The next step will be to ensure that we have the right tools and skills to include in our new system of leading ourselves. We will be covering the most important elements of personal effectiveness, or what I like to call personal mastery, to help us achieve those results identified in our life plan.

"Desire, burning desire, is basic to achieving anything beyond the ordinary."

—Joseph Wirthlin

PERSONAL MASTERY

PREFACE

Peter Sink is a senior lecturer at MIT Sloan School of Management, Leadership, and Sustainability. He defines personal mastery as a set of specific principles and practices that enable a person to learn, create a personal vision, and view the world objectively. Another definition, which I feel is even more relevant, is that it is the process of living and working purposefully toward a vision, in alignment with one's values and in a state of constant learning about oneself and the reality in which one exists. This definition is by Andrew Bryant, a writer for Forbes magazine.

In this chapter, we go over a set of skills that will help us manage our time effectively, place our energy in the right direction, and acquire the right mindset to understand what we need to keep us moving forward to reach our potential and personal greatness.

WHY?

What is the recipe for success in achieving your personal greatness? Is it hard work? Let me tell you my story. Most of the people who have worked with me know that I am very hardworking, and I don't spare any time or effort in order to achieve my goals and complete my tasks and projects on schedule with minimum cost; yet, that was never enough, and I felt frustrated because others were being more widely recognized and getting promoted before me, although I was more hardworking.

Was it due to time management? Time management helps in many things. What might be a time management issue for us? Is it related to prioritization? Is it related to doing more in the same time? Actually, this wasn't the right reason. Does it relate to knowing the right people? This is what I thought might be the reason why I was not being promoted at the time. Well, we all know that knowing the right people and having connections will give you an edge in being considered for a promotion. But it will not give you the respect that you deserve, and people will perceive you as a person who may not be worthy. Is favoritism something that we want to be remembered for? Definitely not. If people believe this is the easiest way to go, then probably this book would not be the right guide for them.

So, what is the right recipe to be on track, to be disciplined and determined to meet your vision, your goal, and build the legacy that you want?

HOW?

First, let's explain the competency framework. As I have been a learning and development specialist all my life, and a globally recognized and certified trainer in leadership and development, I understand that this framework is our bread and butter. All training and learning and development specialists recognize the importance of the competency framework. So, what is competency? It's the ability to do something; this can be a technical skill like project planning or it can be a soft skill, such as effective communication and leadership skills.

The reason we need to talk about this is because competency involves a combination of three things: having the right attitude, the willingness to understand and the ability to apply the learning of training or teaching; then we move to the knowledge; and then the application—which is the skill. All these three must be properly aligned. A person perhaps has the right mindset but they may have a problem in grasping the knowledge. Another challenge may be that you are willing to learn but the environment is not helping you to grasp information. What about the person who has the right mindset and then captures that knowledge, but has no opportunity to apply it? Let's say you learned new software and the software is not installed on your laptop or PC; then the learning will eventually become useless. You can't expect someone to improve his or her presentation skills without providing the proper environment in which they can practice and receive feedback!

These three things combined define a competent person. For all of these to be aligned, everything needs to fall into place. However, the most important thing is the attitude, and this is what we want to focus on while we are learning in this chapter and throughout the book, because if you have the right attitude toward achieving your goals, then you'll be able to achieve them no matter what. We talked about vision: envision yourself, visualize yourself, picture your future state so you are already there; you're taking responsibility, as we discussed earlier, for your actions and your life, and you're willing to walk the walk in order to achieve your goal. So, everything else becomes secondary. Knowledge shouldn't be a problem. You'll find ways to educate yourself, whether through formal training, resources on the Internet, or handbooks. You'll make a way, and you will push yourself to practice, to acquire the skills that you want in order to achieve your dream.

What I want to emphasize is that I am presenting globally recognized tools, steps and systems in this book so you can apply best practices to deliver the best results.

A very effective technique that I practiced and have found very useful is taken from Stephen Covey's Seven Habits of Highly Effective People. Seven Habits has proven to be one of the most well-known tools individuals can use for self-management, to gain mastery, and to become distinguished and successful in their lives and careers. This tool is the one I want to talk about in order to help you achieve personal mastery to help you get what you want and achieve your vision.

Stephen talks about the first habit, which is to be proactive. Being proactive means that you are living an intentional life; we have talked about this already. It helps you focus on becoming accountable for your actions by taking full responsibility for your life, and not blaming the weather, your dog, or anybody or anything else, for that matter. It always gives you an edge when you become proactive; you are always in the lead, and you always decide for yourself—and, perhaps, eventually, for others—how you want to deal with your life. This will be covered later in the book in the "Score Credibility" chapter.

The second habit is to begin with your goal in mind. As mentioned when we discussed establishing your vision (see Chapter 1), you always want to picture yourself three to five years ahead—what you will be doing, achieving, and feeling. When the end result is clear and you can visualize it, you will know where you are going and what needs to be achieved. Sometimes, you might change the route, maybe rearrange the steps, reevaluate the process along the way, but you never change the vision (unless there's something really wrong with it or you've defined something incorrectly). Your vision should be derived from who you are, everything that you have built up for twenty, thirty, or forty years. So, it cannot be something that can be easily neglected. This habit is very powerful; use it to your advantage.

The third habit is to put first things first—basically, prioritization. Prioritize what is important; identify what is urgent, what is less important, and so on and so forth. It will help to give your full attention to important matters and effectively manage your time. I like to refer previously trained leaders to the Johari Window. The Johari Window explains the difference between important and urgent matters and tasks, and describes how we should focus in order to col-laborate well with others, as well as deliver results and take control of our time.

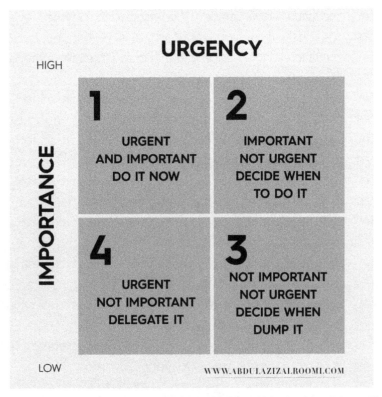

Source: https://www.pinterest.com/4ea7f19849f0a2e3bf7a8c0ddc2cf5/_saved/

The fourth habit is to think "win-win." Not a lot of people think this way. Win-win isn't as clear as it sounds; it doesn't mean that everybody is 100% happy. What it means is that we need to work effectively with others for our mutual benefit. I like to refer to this African proverb:

"If you want to walk fast, walk alone; but if you want to walk far, walk together." I will elaborate on this in the later chapters.

So, people with a win-win mindset realize the impact of giving up some of what they want for the sake of getting something of greater value by focusing on the bigger picture—what really counts. It involves some sacrifice, but nothing too major; otherwise, it will be a win-lose.

The fifth habit is to seek first to understand, then to be understood. It asks us to listen and understand the other person. First, we put ourselves in the other person's shoes because sometimes we see things from our own perspective and we assume things. We think we know the person very well: "Oh, this person will come again with the same excuse, and it happens on a daily basis."

A few months back, I had a challenge with one of my team members who always arrived late to work. One day, he came to me, and I thought he would apologize for being late again, but it turned out that, on that day, he had arrived an hour before everybody else. I almost disciplined him for his bad behavior. Luckily, I restrained myself from giving my employee tough talk because I thought that he had behaved as usual. It is important not to assume things. Everybody has an excuse, whether it's legitimate or not, but everyone deserves to be heard and clearly understood. That's why there is an important behavior and skill that we refer to in training and in coaching, which is "mirroring," also known by the term "active listening." So, you not only listen to the words, but you actually listen with your heart and mind. It shows in your body language that you are really trying to understand the person and what's behind their message in order to genuinely help them with the problem they are facing.

The sixth habit is synergies. Synergies are basically finding people who share the same interests as you. It's similar to win-win; however, win-win is related to negotiation. Synergies is where you seek to work with people who already have similar interests in order to amplify your impact in your job or life; like our fellow author Moustafa Hamwi, who likes to have a "passion tribe," made up of people who share a passion for writing, a passion to be heard and a passion to make a difference in the world. We meet up every once in a while, and we support each other; because we have the same challenges and tasks, we share some of our dreams and aspirations. We support each other in order to keep ourselves motivated and to learn from one another.

The seventh and the last habit, which is crucial and one that I think most people fall short on (including me over the past few years), is sharpen the saw. It tells us that we need to energize ourselves, make ourselves happy and celebrate our achievements. Why do we need that? Because no one will give us credit but ourselves, so we need to give ourselves credit to be fair to ourselves and celebrate our milestones in order to keep moving. Because what we're trying to pursue is not the norm. We are going against the tide. We want to prove ourselves right, and we want to prevail, and we want to compete with other professionals. So, we need to have this fuel that will keep us moving forward.

From a wellness, health, and psychological point of view, everything comes together according to The Seven Habits. (We have also discussed this "Wheel of Life" in the previous chapter.) It's a strong tool; you can always get more information and details about it and how it can be applied to your life.

For The Seven Habits to work effectively for you, and in order to be focused, resilient and determined to achieve your goals, make sure to have the following:

A positive mindset. You will always need to look at the brighter side of any situation and always believe that you can do it; this is essential. This positive mentality can push us from "I Want to do it," to "I Can do it!" while enjoying the process of change and facing the challenges along the way.

Ability to overcome adversity. These two points I learned from a webinar by Mr. John Boe. I think these points come together as enablers for The Seven Habits. You need to expect challenges and reversals from time to time. No one says when you apply The Seven Habits, or any other method of personal development, everything will go perfectly; you will continue to face problems, and it takes time to be comfortable in your new behaviors. We expect hardship, and we need to support ourselves with the right positive mindset, reapply the tools, and raise the bar further and further for our skills and competencies to achieve our goals.

LESSONS LEARNED

In this chapter, we covered the skills that will help us manage our time effectively, place our energy in the right direction, and have the right mindset to keep us moving forward. We have also touched on The Seven Habits as a recommended vehicle that we can acquire in order to achieve our goals with the right mindset and determination.

CALL FOR ACTION

Now you can evaluate yourself on the nine principles. These are The Seven Habits plus the principles of keeping a positive mindset and overcoming adversity. The recommended method for self-evaluation is to rate yourself in each one on a scale from one to ten. Then identify which one or two of the nine characteristics you need to improve on the most.

As for the mindset, if you don't have the right attitude—in other words, if it's less than a nine or a ten—then it will not be sufficient for you to succeed. You will have problems because it's the foundation of everything else; and if it's shaky, then the base for everything else is not solid. So, you need to reevaluate and ask yourself why you did not rate it as a nine or a ten.

What do you think is an acceptable number when you rate yourself from one to ten on all nine elements? Anything that rates below seven should be an area of concern. Perhaps you have a problem with time; maybe you have a problem with win-win negotiation; it could be that you have a lot of conflict with others; maybe you're too passive and wait for other people to take action on your behalf. So, you need to keep all nine principles rated above seven, and then hope that they will all reach nine in order for you to do things right and achieve what you want. Because whatever problem you have now, remember that it's only related to you. When you become responsible for others as a future or a current leader, the problem will double or triple.

I like this quote from Trenton, who is part of LinkedIn: "97% of people who quit too soon are employed by the 3% who didn't."

So, discipline is very crucial at this stage of one's personal mastery. Here, I refer to the Golden Principles of Marshall Goldsmith, and they are courage, humility, and discipline. You need to be courageous, be proactive, take responsibility, and have humility because life will put you down. You don't know when, but you know the obstacle is coming, and then you need to get back up and continue moving forward and doing what you promised yourself and others you'd do. That is discipline.

Since you have equipped yourself with the right capabilities to manage yourself and have obtained personal mastery, and you are ready to pursue your personal greatness, you need to take it to the next level: influencing others. And that's what we'll discuss in the next chapter.

CHAPTER 3

FORMULA OF INFLUENCE

"Leaders establish trust with candor, transparency, and credit."

—Jack Welch

SCORE CREDIBILITY

PREFACE

This chapter covers what John Adair describes as the top qualities of an credible leader in his famous book Leadership and Motivation. These qualities are as follows:

Integrity: what it means, how it affects others, and how important it is to have integrity in order to be perceived as a credible person and a leader.

Enthusiasm: how we can use it as a powerful tool to impact others.

Humility: how it affects others and helps us to be seen as authentic leaders.

Two important supporting qualities are: courage and perseverance.

How can this mix help us earn credibility in front of others so that they will want to follow us?

WHY?

Integrity is perceived as the most important quality by most if not all leadership and management gurus. I have personally heard it from John Adair when he delivered a live session about his book The Leadership of Muhammad in Kuwait. He talked about the different qualities of Prophet Muhammad—peace be upon him—describing him as a highly credible, influential, and successful leader. When he summed up, he said that the number one or most important quality that distinguished Prophet Muhammad—peace upon him—from the rest of the leaders was integrity! Integrity is critical. It needs to be practiced every day, in every action, which can be challenging for most people. As humans, we are most likely to compromise our integrity because, sometimes, we get mixed feelings, our mood affects our decision-making, and there are other elements and aspects that can negatively affect our integrity. Even if we are doing the right things, people might perceive our actions differently. Integrity makes people trust us. The more integrity we have and demonstrate—whether to colleagues, team members, or clients—and the more we do things the right way, the more trust we will have from the people around us and the people we work with, including clients and stakeholders.

Enthusiasm is important because, as a leader, you need to bring new ideas, thoughts, and initiatives that excite you and your followers or team. In order for you to get buy-in from the team, the ideas need to excite them too; so the first thing they need to see from you is your own enthusiasm about the idea. This is part of the selling technique as well as how to market such thoughts. However, there is a right balance between energetic enthusiasm and being perceived as a credible, mature, and logical person. We'll be discussing this later on.

The last quality is humility. Humility is captivating. People relate to a person with this quality. Most of the people in this world are facing challenges and are always looking for a leader who will guide them toward a better life and a better world. When considering whether to choose you as a leader, they will look for integrity, enthusiasm, and humility because they know this will make them enthusiastic as well—and if you are humble, you can feel what they feel and be a role model because you have walked the walk. I will explain further how to obtain this quality and use it in a business setting.

HOW?

What is integrity? Well, the definition of integrity is "the quality of being honest and having strong moral principles" and "the state of being whole and undivided" (Oxford English Dictionary). Both definitions clearly explain what integrity really means in a simple way. Essentially, integrity tells us that we need to be honest with ourselves and with others, and we need to demonstrate this honesty with everything that we do. When people see you as fair and just, and you are displaying your values and your beliefs, then you will be perceived as a person with integrity.

Let me share an example of poor integrity and how it can destroy your career. I will take the example of Enron.

For many decades, Enron was a globally prominent, well-known, successful organization; then it all collapsed following a major episode of fraud. Even with a complete change of leadership, nobody was willing to place his or her trust in the company anymore; it wasn't salvageable. So, losing integrity means losing yourself! How can I preserve my personal and organizational integrity? You need to build confidence, and to build confidence, you need to be realistic about what you preach and keep in mind how critical it is to maintain such virtue. According to Warren Buffett, one of the most successful investors of all time, "It takes twenty years to build a reputation and five minutes to ruin it. If you think about that, you'll do things differently."

Living with integrity helps us live a simple and logical life because you don't need to convince yourself that you're doing the right thing; you already know it. You make decisions based on your values and what you think is right, and then live with the consequences; that's the quality of a leader. A leader does the right thing. According to Peter Drucker, the influential thinker on strategic management, "Leaders do the right things, while managers do things right." So, you do what you think and you believe is correct and continue with your life.

To build and enhance your integrity, you need to acknowledge it in your daily life. Encourage others to show it and build a system to maintain it. Not many people have sufficient self-confidence or self-esteem to maintain their integrity. To enhance or acquire that skill, we need to be clear on what matters for us, what our core values are; then we rank these things based on their importance. For example, if you want to make a decision on whether to leave a job or oppose your direct manager's decision because it goes against your values and you believe it is wrong or unacceptable, then you need to raise that issue and stand up for your values.

Your values shouldn't do any harm to others. Your beliefs should focus only on doing well and bringing good things to others; for example, believing in equality and fairness, etc.

Once you decide to take action, you always need to come up with options, evaluate and select the most suitable option, and make appropriate decisions. Remember not to live "larger than life" and to be logical and realistic about the conditions. So, don't start a war if your values have been impacted or abused. From your point of view, you are one person out of seven billion plus. You just need to step away from that environment because it's only going to make you miserable. Always follow and work with people who have very strong integrity so that you will also be part of this group and this mindset. This will nurture your integrity and your values. You need to continue developing your personal mastery in order to be in control of your life; then your voice will be heard, and your opinions will be more respected and appreciated.

The next quality is enthusiasm. Enthusiasm is critical for any leader to acquire. Why? It's because you're dealing with people, and people are a mixture of emotions and logic; maybe more emotions than logic for many (people who work in marketing know that very well). Sometimes, people go to a stadium to watch a football match although they could watch it at home where they would be more comfortable on their sofas; they are seeking to share in the enthusiasm along with other fans. That's what makes them go there and live the moment. This is especially true in times of celebration. People are enthusiastic and happy when they're celebrating their achievements.

However, you need the right amount; having too much or too little enthusiasm is dangerous. This can be crucial and can have a negative impact on your influence as a leader or on the message you're sharing with your audience. For example, if your idea is to introduce a new practice or product or change your organization's way of working, then your team should see that your level of enthusiasm is appropriate to the impact you want to deliver. In contrast, if the activity can be done within a few weeks, then its impact is going to be minimal. You might not show much excitement there because then you would be exaggerating. Showing more enthusiasm than is actually required means that you are underestimating the quality of the team members and, at the same time, overestimating the impact. This can lead your team to see you as selfish because it creates an impression that all you care about is your accomplishments. This will make others see you as someone who is too immature or inexperienced to realize the real size of the accomplishment.

You need to weigh the impact of your decisions and channel your enthusiasm where it really matters because leadership is about impact and results. You need to find that sweet balance between exaggerating and underselling your idea to others and yourself as well.

An example of enthusiasm—maybe a little bit exaggerated, but I still like the example—is Diego Maradona, the Argentinian football legend. While he had a problem with discipline, he was very charismatic, and many people believe that he was one of the best players in history. Whenever you saw him on the bench, being the coach or the manager of a team, you saw all the energy in the stadium. His enthusiasm and energy were contagious. Another example is Jose Mourinho, the Portuguese coach and manager of a different European top football club; he is also very well-known for energizing his teams and keeping them motivated.

So, these are the two examples that I like to refer to when talking about enthusiasm. The difference is that Mourinho has backed it up with great accomplishments as a coach while Maradona failed in this role. This makes Mourinho the more credible coach and leader.

Let us shed more light on humility. As I said, humility makes people want to be with us and around us because it's the opposite of arrogance. When you are arrogant, you are mean and you see yourself as better than others. There's no harm in developing yourself, but that does not give you the right to look down upon others. People appreciate your credentials, accomplishments, education, and qualities when you deal with them as human beings and treat them with respect and are willing to learn and listen to others without displaying your authority or experience; they appreciate your humbleness. Maintaining a balance between humility and ego will help you stay humble and not become arrogant; that's where the magic lies. People would prefer to work with someone more influential and impactful because it will help them to be better. A humble person doesn't show that they are superior and doesn't deal with others in a dismissive way. Rather, they behave with dignity toward themselves and others while working together.

Keep in mind you need to maintain a constant level of humility and integrity, irrespective of whether you are dealing with a stakeholder or not, and that's what you should be known for. A good example I have in mind is Sir Richard Branson, owner of many companies including Virgin Airlines. Basically, Sir Richard Branson is always seen working side by side with his employees. He's very proud of them, and you can see that he does not place himself above his employees. He's more about empowering them and expects greatness from them. If you ask anyone who observes Sir Richard Branson, you would learn that he hopes that his employees are more successful than him; at least that's my perception.

Now we'll talk about what it means to be courageous. Courage is critical for anyone who wants to leave a mark on the world. If you want to live with integrity, if you want to be perceived as an enthusiastic and humble leader, then you have to be courageous. If you have nothing to offer, challenge, or aspire to, you cannot claim that you are courageous. You have to walk the walk so people want to follow you; they want to follow someone they perceive as a hero. Can you think of any heroes known for being cowards? A hero usually has their own fears and they overcome them for their own sake and for the sake of others, for a greater purpose.

I like this quote by Napoleon Bonaparte: "If you build an army of lions and their leader is a dog, in any fight, the lions will die like dogs. But if you build an army of dogs and their leader is a lion, all dogs will fight like a lion." I read this quote every day when I'm leading my team, and I remind myself every single day to be a lion. Not surprisingly, lions have integrity and pride, and they have the right amount of enthusiasm. They have courage and, of course, they have the next element as well, which is perseverance.

Sylvester Stallone, as the character Rocky Balboa, had some advice for his son: "Let me tell you something you already know. The world isn't all sunshine and rainbows. It is a very mean and nasty place. And I don't care how tough you are, it will beat you to your knees and keep you there permanently if you let it. You, I, and nobody is going to hit as hard as life." Well said, Mr. Stallone. This guy embodies the virtue of "perseverance." Everybody knows the actor Sylvester Stallone, but probably not everyone knows his story. He has spent his life suffering and striving to reach where he is—one of Hollywood's superstars. He had his challenges in acting. He has semi-paralyzed face muscles that prevent him from speaking well. He wrote his own movie, took care of himself for the Rocky series and found success. This element of the plot shows the integrity of Stallone: even in his own movie, the first of the series, his character lost the big fight, or actually it was a draw with his competitor, Apollo Creed. So, that was the "aha" moment; what made this movie special and how did he see life? "It's not only about winning; it's about continuing to pursue your dreams and believing in yourself because no one else will." — Rocky Balboa, Or at least even if they believe in you, you are the number one believer in yourself and the greatness that you have and the potential that you see in yourself.

CONDITIONS FOR SUCCESS

To have integrity, you have to be a role model according to your values. Don't overpromise and then under-deliver. You need to walk the walk and lead by example, show people what integrity means, and stick to your values. To be enthusiastic, you need to follow your vision and values. This is the only way to show how important it is for you and for others.

To have humility, you need to do the hard work and value others for who they are, not for their titles.

Mary Kay Ash, founder of Mary Kay Cosmetics, said it beautifully: "We treat our people like royalty. If you honor and serve the people who work for you, they will honor and serve you." So, we need to treat people with respect in order for them to treat us with respect.

Do you have the courage to master these three qualities—integrity, enthusiasm, and humility? If so, how long will it take you to master them and maintain them over time? The answer should be that you will master and practice these three skills for the rest of your life.

LESSONS LEARNED

We covered the qualities of a credible person and leader, and we discussed how important integrity is and how it impacts others. Then we talked about enthusiasm—how to spread it to others and how to balance it to be perceived as positive and not immature. Humility—the thin line between humility and humiliation, and ego and the sweet spot in the middle—was also explained. We now also realize why and how one should be courageous, and how we can persevere and maintain our commitment to achieve our life vision and impact others.

CALL FOR ACTION

What is the most important value among these three attributes from your point of view? Is it integrity, humility, or enthusiasm? What do you think you need to work on first? What do you need to do or continue doing to be perceived as a person and a leader with integrity? What actions do you need to do for others to see that you have humility and dignity? How can you balance your enthusiasm to motivate and engage others?

The next topic we'll be discussing is how to be perceived as an authority. This will help you to know how to market yourself, show your qualities and your experience, build your personal brand, gain followers through your charisma, and be seen as a person who is capable of leading others.

SOURCES

https://digital.com/blog/leadership-quotes/
https://knowledge.wharton.upenn.edu/article/lessons-in-leadership-from-the-life-of-the-prophet-muhammad/
John Adair, 2009, Leadership and Motivation
John Adair, 2010, The Leadership of Muhammad

"The greatest ability in business is to get along with others and influence their actions."

—John Hancock

BE AN AUTHORITY

PREFACE

In this chapter, we will elaborate on how you can be perceived as an authority by building an effective personal brand. We will discuss how to be known and seen by your audience, and what qualities are expected, respected, and admired by others, along with how to build and enhance your own charisma with the knowledge and expertise to lead and influence others.

WHY?

"Personal brand is what people say about you when you are not in the room." This is what personal branding means to Jeff Bezos, the CEO of Amazon. So, a personal brand is what other people think of you, feel about you, and expect from you. You will be judged on what you say and do, whether you are aware of it or not. It is important to realize this and take care that what you say in public, the workplace and on social media reflects the values and characteristics that you want to be known for. To be an influential leader, you need to have the right personal brand and understand what that really means.

John Adair discusses the qualities that we'll talk about: being respected and admired by others. There are four elements involved: you need to be a person of knowledge; you need to know how to deal with people; you need to have the right decision-making tools in order to succeed in aiding others; and you need to have charisma. Why do we need charisma? Can you imagine an effective leader who lacks charisma? We will explain how to obtain and enhance your personal charisma to help you to achieve your vision.

HOW?

Let us start with the personal brand. Joseph Liu from Forbes explains personal brand as follows: "It is a way to establish and enhance who you are, what you stand for in your career and life. Everything you do either strengthens or weakens the personal brand you are trying to create." So, your personal brand reflects what you stand for, what you live for, what you admire, and how you want people to perceive you. You need to focus on your strengths and the value you bring to society, your clients, and the world. Yes, the world—thanks to the Internet, your product or service can be valuable to others on the other side of the globe.

This is a general definition of the importance of a personal brand. If we think again about Sir Richard Branson, we recall that he is a person who has humility and who likes to have fun. He has demonstrated that he is a caring leader; he is very adventurous, and he lives his life on the go. If we look at Steve Jobs—he is well-known for his innovation. That was clear in all of his speeches and products. He was also a huge supporter of the idea of following your passion. This is what we mean when talking about a personal brand.

Returning to Elon Musk again—he is known for changing the world. He wants people to live on Mars in the future; he is a part of that movement, and his companies are actually working on it. This is the kind of mentality and personal brand that he is known for.

It is clear that we can build and enhance our personal brand and make other people notice us for that brand by recognizing our strengths, our values, and our vision.

Joseph Liu lists some practical tips to enhance our personal brand:

Number one: say yes to relevant opportunities. For example, a programmer can be tagged as the "data guy," which builds a brand that you are an introvert and do not work well with others!

I personally have been perceived as a person who has an innovative and creative mind; that was certainly the case when I worked at EQUATE. I've been told over and over again that "EQUATE wasn't the right place for innovation at that time because we were in the manufacturing sector where safety is the number one priority, so we needed to follow our process religiously." However, things have changed now because innovation is a crucial skill and mindset that we need to adopt for the future. But at the time, in order for me to change the perception that I was only a person of innovation (because innovation comes with risk-taking and thinking independently; those are good traits, but not a good match for the culture at that time) I had to show them that I was very responsible and keen on mitigating risk, and that I could follow through very well on the established process. I had to be engaged in any opportunity to help show that I could follow procedures. So, I got involved and was one of the very first people in my department to get Green Belt Six Sigma, which is all about following the process.

So, say yes to relevant opportunities in order to show your skills and get away from the tag that people give to you, unless you're okay with it.

Number two: speak at a conference. In fact, it doesn't have to be a conference. Any public gathering, formal or informal, is a suitable venue for you to share your thoughts. Let people know who you are and what you're good at—not necessarily your main strength! It could be your second strength; for example, if you're good with data and you also want to be known for effective problem solving, speak about that, and let people see that you have more than one strength to add to the organization and to the team.

Number three: ask one question at every meeting you attend. Be engaged and realize where you can intervene in the area that is of the most interest to you. Make sure that you ask a question that is meaningful and reflects your area or angle of thinking so that you add your point of view for the complete understanding of the group.

Number four: network internally beyond your immediate team. We discussed this in the previous chapter when we talked about synergies; it will benefit you later to let people know more about you. My personal story would be that I pride myself on being a hard worker. I have always been a hard worker, and I give a lot of focus to completing all my pending work. When I networked, other people observed and noticed what I am capable of; it built more trust among my peers. While building my network, I started sharing more of my personal interests, such as hobbies and my love of history. It helped me find better opportunities to shine and to be known for different qualities, such as public speaking. Morgan Chaney, the head of marketing at BlueBoard.com says, "The internal networking and the relationship building is critical to building your personal brand."

Number five: share your voice with influencers. One of the best ways to amplify your personal brand is to participate in radio shows, write in the newspaper, become active on social media or even become an influencer on that plat-form. You can also collaborate with internal influencers and decision-makers who can give you a project that will have the right impact. For example, in 2016, I had the opportunity to go on a radio show, and I talked about leadership. A lot of people from my organization heard about it. Although I didn't really market my radio talk internally, they knew about it and listened to the interview; they didn't realize that I had that potential and that much knowledge about this topic. Ever since, I have been regarded as a person with knowledge, a person with authority. I believe it helped me get an "Outstanding Performance" in my performance appraisal that year.

Another personal example—when the happiness program at EQUATE was introduced, I was one of the first people recommended by my direct manager and my senior manager for this team. This was because it reflected part of my values: working with others, collaborating, teamwork, and making people feel valued and happy. First, I was an engaged team member; then, eventually, I led the team and changed the scope from Corporate Wellness to Employee Wellness to the Employee Happiness Program. At that time, my colleagues at EQUATE realized that I had many interests, technical expertise, and passions. I had another opportunity where I was the MC at the farewell for an EQUATE CEO, which was an enjoyable experience both for me and for the audience. So, by practicing and sharing your expertise with colleagues and having the right network to promote yourself in, you will strengthen your personal band.

What I'd like to close this part with is that if you don't define your personal brand, others will do it for you, and not always in a way that you would choose!

Now let's talk about charisma. The word "charisma" is Greek in origin; it means "the gift of God" or "the preference of the divine." It can indicate that a person has a great attraction and overwhelming presence. There is another definition, however, which is "the ability to influence people culturally or emotionally through personal charm or extraordinary power or authority." A charismatic person is easily remembered and recognized. Charisma can involve the way you speak or act; it doesn't have a specific scope. For example, when we talk about active listening, there is a set of behaviors you need to demonstrate to do it fully. When we talk about presentation skills and body language, there is a right way and a wrong way to do it; there is no in-between. When it comes to charisma, you cannot decide to have it; it's either part of your DNA or developed over time. Charismatic leaders such as Steve Jobs, Sir Richard Branson, Martin Luther King, Muhammad Ali, or Denzel Washington, although they are different in style and their achievements are in different fields, are captivating and influential. The way I perceive it is that it's about power. There is an authority behind this person's words. It's not how they look, talk, or even what they say. Charismatic people are perceived as being knowledgeable and experienced and as having a real value that contributes to others, and that's what gives them that power. They are always sure of their actions and hopes for the future. They can push people to move. They force people to listen to them. They command attention; they have all of this. Deep inside, I feel that they have the four qualities of a credible person (which we'll cover shortly).

Having charisma is a double-edged sword. People either like you or hate you. Your charisma is what makes you different. Expect your audience either to get engaged in a positive way or a negative way; your audiences will either like you or they won't. Either way, you will command their attention. People will listen to you, no matter what you say. Then if you expect people to listen to you, you should expect to have followers and supporters who agree with your vision or idea, and that there will also be those who disagree and oppose you! Why oppose you? Because you are influential, and if what you're saying conflicts with their own beliefs and interests, then you become a threat! So keep that in the back of your mind when deciding when to be charismatic and when to keep a low profile (if you can).

Last but not least, we will talk about the fact that knowledge is power. What knowledge are we talking about? The first type is people knowledge, the general knowledge of how to understand people and what motivates them, according to John Adair's book Leadership and Motivation. Leaders acquire this knowledge and understand how to deal with people. The second type of knowledge is the "know-how." Leaders acquire good information of the topic under consideration; they are not necessarily experts in this field, but they have very good knowledge of what they're talking about. People perceive them as experts; their colleagues respect them and take them seriously because they are confident about their knowledge. Still, they will gather people in their team who have more expertise in order to accomplish the daily operational or specific tasks.

There is another challenge that you need to be aware of. If you know too much and you are a subject matter expert in a topic, then this is a dangerous position to be in, especially when leading teams. Because your team members will see that you are the expert and can do it all by yourself, they may not be sure that their work will meet your expectations, or even understand why they are in the team. Then, most likely, you will fall into the trap of doing things on your own because you are playing the roles of the leader, consultant, and expert.

As a follow-up to the technical trap—if you want to be a leader, you need to be careful not to be tagged as the technician or the technical guy or the specialist in this area. Usually, leaders are well-rounded, and have a more general expertise when leading teams or projects. If you want to lead in the future, play more of a general role on a more strategic level so you will not be cornered or tagged as the technical specialist. There will be some managers who may be afraid to give you the opportunity because then they lose your experience and expertise; they'd rather keep you there to make sure that operations are going well.

Another element of know-how is decision-making. Effective decision-making helps the group find solutions through problem solving and creative thinking. A leader needs to know how to deal with conflict, how to make decisions, how to keep people engaged, etc. This complements their people knowledge.

Last but not least is the knowledge about leadership and management, which we'll touch on later in the book. We have wrapped up the part related to the qualities of a leader who is respected and admired by others. I want to end with a quote on the crucial impact of knowledge: "Authority flows to him who knows."

CONDITIONS FOR SUCCESS

In order to have a strong personal brand and to be an authority, you must define what you want to be known for and also know what your strengths are: your first strength, your second strength, third strength, and maybe fourth. If you want to be known by others, then you need to be courageous because you will be put on the spot and people will have to defend your point. Maybe they will doubt you. So, you need to have that courage because you want to be visible to the world and in your organization. You need to be sure that you have the right knowledge, that whatever you say is correct, and that you are positive about your information. You are putting yourself on the spot, so be credible. To be an authority, you need to follow through and cover all that we have mentioned, as well as have the self-confidence to build and enhance your charisma; then people won't doubt what you say or do. Make sure things look good on paper: strong resume, good list of accomplishments, clear writing, insightful comments and thoughts, and, hopefully, good results. Remember that you want to influence and inspire your stakeholders. All these skills can be practiced and mastered; you need to think this through and have the courage to be out there and share your personal brand with the world.

CALL FOR ACTION

Here are additional tips to grow your personal brand from Joseph Liu:

Tip number one: complete an audit of your projects on your own and with your manager to align and focus on those that best reinforce the personal brand you are trying to build.

Tip number two: volunteer to share a project update at any upcoming meeting or conference that reinforces an area of expertise you want to be known for.

Tip number three: at your next meeting, make a point to ask a relevant question related to your expertise that helps deepen the discussion or clarify a particular topic for you and others.

Tip number four: reconnect with one colleague outside your immediate work area to learn more about their current priorities and discuss potential ways you could help one another based on your specific areas of expertise.

As for knowledge and qualities—first, we need to balance and evaluate how well we are doing with the four qualities and be more engaged and raise the bar for our qualities compared to other team members so that we can be more influential; then charisma will follow.

We have completed the section concerned with how to be a person of authority, distinguished among your competitors, influencers, or the team that you want to influence. I will provide you with a set of techniques, skills, and tools that will help you command attention, build and enhance your charisma through the power of words, and use your emotional intelligence in a way that will make other people like and accept you.

SOURCES

https://navidmoazzez.com/best-personal-branding-quotes/
https://www.forbes.com/sites/josephliu/2018/04/30/personal-brand-work/#6d0cd31b7232

"Be so good that they can't ignore you."

—Steve Martin

COMMUNICATE WITH IMPACT

PREFACE

In this chapter, you will be able to learn secrets and techniques that are globally recognized and practiced. These skills will make other people like you and trust you; then follow you.

You will learn essential techniques of emotional intelligence, which can help you in building your brand. We will also talk about Dale Carnegie's Golden Principles, which are outlined in How to Win Friends and Influence People, one of the best-selling books of all time on human relations, to help you build more productive relationships so you can achieve your vision.

We will also tap into powerful speaking techniques that will allow you to impact others.

WHY?

Let's start with emotional intelligence, and let's see what Jack Welch, former CEO of General Electric, has to say about it Welch says, "No doubt emotional intelligence is rarer than book smarts, but my experience says it is actually more important in the making of a leader; you just can't ignore it."

So, what is emotional intelligence? According to the definition on Mindtools.com, it is "the ability to understand and manage your own emotions so you can better know yourself and the emotions of the people around you and others. People with a high degree of emotional intelligence know what they are feeling, what their emotions mean, and how these emotions can affect other people."

So, why do we need self-awareness? Well, before people can trust us, they need to like us and accept us. We can't get them to do this if we don't know what our shortfalls or shortcomings are, how we are perceived, how we look, how we communicate, whether people feel comfortable around us, and so forth. Gaining trust is a question of behaving in a trustworthy way. Self-awareness is key for us to improve ourselves and help others.

Then why do we need to build productive relationships? We all have many relationships—we can socialize all day—but do they all really count? Are we socializing with the right people? Whether we want to find business leads, make connections to increase our influence and our visibility, or enhance our personal brand, we need to learn who the right people are to know and work with in order for us to achieve our goals.

Another essential factor is the power of words. Why is that important? Basically, if you want people to do something, you need to communicate your desires effectively; this entails verbal communication and body language. So, we will focus on what we need to do for people to like us, be happy around us, and do what we want them to do without manipulation or faking anything. When your motives are authentic, your communication is both more genuine and more effective.

HOW?

When we realize how our emotions affect the people around us, we understand the need for high emotional intelligence and effective management of our emotions. For example, some people get irritated easily or are quick to get angry; maybe they don't pay attention when someone is talking to them. These traits might send the wrong message. Although these emotions might be genuine, they don't project the image or message that you want your peers to receive.

Increasing your emotional intelligence will help you to be more influential, first, by making your colleagues and team members like you and want to work with you. You will also learn what behaviors you need to change and what behaviors you need to improve in order to be accepted by others.

Sounds good, doesn't it? With a greater understanding of our emotions, we can build positive and productive relationships with other people, which will eventually help us in our professional lives and personal lives. Let us see how to improve our emotional intelligence.

Dr. Daniel Goleman from Harvard University divided emotional intelligence into four elements:

Number one is self-awareness, which includes the ability to know yourself and understand your feelings, understand and recognize your strengths and weaknesses, and have confidence and faith in yourself.

Number two is self-management or how well you control your emotions. This includes how you work and manage yourself and achieve your goals, whether you have initiative, you are self-motivated, you're honest and open and transparent so you're perceived as being trustworthy, you're adaptable and have resilience, you have an optimistic mindset, or whether you have a positive outlook in life.

Number three is social awareness. The first two elements are related to understanding yourself; the second two are related to understanding other people. So, social awareness has two points. The first is empathy, the degree to which we understand and acknowledge others' emotions. Are we aware of what other people are feeling? The other is helpfulness; are we contributing to the group effort, or are we just pretending to listen?

Number four is relationship management. Are we perceived as good mentors? Are we perceived as authority figures? As role models? Do we influence and motivate others? Do we know how to manage conflict? Are we a catalyst for change? Are we good at developing the strengths and talents of others? Do we have a good sense of teamwork, and are we collaborative?

Particularly for social awareness and relationship management, in general, extroverts have an edge because these are traits aligned with their natural preferences and their experience; they are already more social than introverts. So, usually, it is easier for extroverts to equip themselves with these skills. But that doesn't mean people who are naturally introverted can't learn to cultivate and improve in these areas. As you can see, emotional intelligence involves a variety of subjects that cover and manage our relationships, and help us understand how we can make them impactful in a positive way.

I would like to talk about Dale Carnegie's 30 Golden Principles. I'm not going to cover all the principles in his well-known book How to Win Friends and Influence People. I'm a Dale Carnegie certified trainer, and I have followed his teachings with my group here in Kuwait for the past five years. We will, however, talk about the main points and principles related to working with and influencing people.

The first set that we will go through is techniques for handling people:
- Don't criticize, condemn, or complain.
- Give honest and sincere appreciation.
- Arouse in the other person an eager want.

Next, we're going to talk about six ways to make people like you:
- Smile... Yes, just smile!

- Become genuinely interested in other people. "Genuinely" is the key word. We always talk about being genuine and authentic; it's true. No faking or manipulation here!
- Remember that a person's name is, to that person, the sweetest and the most important sound in any language. Dale Carnegie mentions that he couldn't memorize the names of everyone he met, so he kept notes about their full names and other personal information, maybe including dates of birth and things they liked. So, because this technique made other people happy and made Dale Carnegie happy, he kept a note of that, and he kept calling people every once in a while, referring to them by their full name. It's something that makes people feel valued and appreciated.
- Be a good listener. Encourage others to talk about themselves.
- Talk in terms of the other person's interests. Sometimes when people want to start a conversation, they never stop talking and they jump from one topic to the other. If we just listen and we let people feel comfortable enough to talk about themselves, they will automatically feel happier talking to us.
- Make the other person feel important, and do it sincerely. So, in order for us to become important, we need to make the other person feel important. This is one of the mottos I live by in my life. I always tell myself that if I want to be important, I need to make others feel that way first. A simple example: if I attend a funeral for my friend or a colleague and someone sees me there who didn't expect me to attend, he will appreciate the

gesture. The next time he sees me, he will give me special treatment. He will perceive me as a special person; although I may not want anything in return, I made him feel valuable. This is how you make yourself feel valuable as well.

The other set of Golden Principles is categorized as how to Win People to Your Way of Thinking. These are points to transform others to do things that we want:

- The only way to get the best of an argument is to avoid it.
- Show respect for the other person's opinion and never say they are wrong.
- If you are wrong, admit it quickly and emphatically. So, there is no ego; you're being selfless here in dealing with others.
- Begin in a friendly way.
- Get another person to say "yes, yes" immediately.
- Let the other person do most of the talking (this also matches number five in "The Six Ways to Make People Like You").
- Let the other person feel that the idea is theirs.
- Try honestly to see things from the other person's point of view. The key word here is "honestly." We need to put ourselves in the other person's position to the greatest extent possible. A key part of this skill is listening to understand, not just to respond.
- Be sympathetic to the other person's ideas and desires. This aligns with the previous points that state we need to be supportive to people struggling to share their ideas.

- Appeal to the nobler motives.
- Dramatize your ideas. This is related to communication.
- Throw down a challenge. Once you talk about a challenge, people will be motivated and excited because they're being challenged to do something.

Now, we will talk about the third point to command attention, which is speaking with confidence. We may know what to say, but we might not know the best way to say it; this is key for making the right impact. Meryl Runion's book How to Use the Power of Phrases lists Six Steps to Command Attention. These include the following:

The first step is to be brief. In order to have a powerful communication, we need to be brief.

The second step is to be specific.

I like the quote by Plato: "Wise men speak because they have something to say; fools speak because they have to say something." So, silence is golden—not all the time, but when you do speak, be brief and to the point.

The third step is to speak with an end in mind—talk about outcomes. It's also mentioned as one of The Seven Habits we talked about earlier. So, tell people what the end results are so that people can visualize what you're talking about.

The fourth step is to tell the truth; say what you feel, what you think, and what you want. So, if you're not happy with something, just say so. If you have a thought in your mind, just spit it out and tell it. You don't need to keep it to yourself; you already know it, but it's the other person that needs to know it.

The fifth step is never promise what you can't or won't deliver. This is related to your integrity. We talked about being genuine. Don't be caught up in the moment or the emotions and say things that you don't mean or you cannot deliver (over promise).

The sixth step is don't be mean. Be fair and objective. Sometimes we need to say things that we don't want to say, such as when firing someone or punishing someone or coaching someone for bad behavior. Make sure to be objective, and always remember that when we deliver feedback, our coaching should focus not on the person but on the behavior or the action that was taken. So, if you're going to say something that is tough, don't make it worse by making it personal as well.

These are the six secrets described by Meryl Runion to Make an Impactful and Powerful Communication.

Meryl says: "When you pick your words, create two goals. One goal will be what you want listeners to do. The second goal will be a relationship goal, how you want the relationship to look like when all is said and done."

This sums up how we want our communication to be. It's all about the impact that we want to bring to others—what we want to be remembered for. So, let's always make sure that our relationships are not affected by our communication. We need to be objective so that the message addresses the action or activity, not the person.

Before ending this part, I'd like to mention the impact of communication with an Arnold Schwarzenegger quote from Terminator: "I'll be back." It's brief and it's direct; it has emotional power. This is one of the most famous Hollywood quotes of all time. Brevity can be powerful, as evidenced in many different quotes from different celebrities and public figures such as Martin Luther King's famous line, "I have a dream."

What we say reflects who we are, and it sticks, so we need to choose our words wisely! We know exactly how people perceive us from our words. As said earlier, I encourage you to speak in conferences and become more of a public figure so people will recognize you for who you are and what you're good at. You can imagine, then, that people might judge you for the rest of your life for a short speech that you deliver. If you don't choose your words correctly or you don't prepare for your speech, people may judge your presentation negatively, so keep that in mind.

CONDITIONS FOR SUCCESS

In order to succeed, you need to remember that being genuine is key; don't be fake or manipulative. Also, listen to understand, not to reply. Take your time. Even if you're upset, even if you think you know this person or believe that this person is getting on your nerves, and no matter how clearly you think that the other person is wrong and you are right—this is your image, and you have a greater goal. Don't waste your opportunities by not controlling your emotions. Now that you're more aware of emotional intelligence, you have a tool to manage yourself and to get people to like you and accept you. By better managing yourself, you can manage others and influence them.

Also, remember that actions speak louder than words. No matter what you say and how you say it, people see your behavior and they will know whether you have integrity. They will match your words and beliefs with your deeds, or notice whether you say one thing and do something else. If you demonstrate the right behavior, then even if you are not as good as you want to be as a speaker or as a presenter, your message will still be heard. According to Dr. Albert Mehrabian studies on communication, more than 60% of a speaker's intent is observed through nonverbal and body language. So, your body language will speak on your behalf!

The last point I want to make regarding body language and how it applies to your stakeholders is highlighted in a quote by Peter Drucker: "The most important thing in communication is to hear what isn't being said." So, this is not related to your body language, but to the other person's body language. Maybe they have come to you for comfort. Maybe they are embarrassed. Maybe they are shy. Maybe they have a problem that they cannot say out loud, and their words do not match their physical state. So, this requires you to go the extra mile and really read between the lines and try to figure out what this person is feeling. So, in order to influence others, maybe you don't have to say much; caring for others and being genuine is a powerful communication tool all on its own.

LESSONS LEARNED

In this chapter, you have learned techniques on how to be likable, accepted, and influential by using the Golden Principles and the emotional intelligence theory. This should help you work collectively with others, build productive relationships that will work for you, and use words of impact that will make people do what you want.

CALL FOR ACTION

Now that you have covered these powerful steps and techniques, which are globally practiced, what you need to do is the following:

First, go over the four steps of emotional intelligence. Evaluate yourself, see what you are missing, and check what areas you need to work on. Start applying these skills in your life to achieve your vision.

Second, start practicing the Golden Principles. If you need a tip, use one each day. Embrace these valuable principles set forth by Dale Carnegie; we can memorize them and coach each other on demonstrating them or bring it to each other's attention when we are not demonstrating them. So, it is crucial that we live by them, especially while we're training and communicating with each other as Dale Carnegie colleagues and trainers. These principles have been proven to work for more than eighty years in different cultures and different languages. I recommend that you practice them and you learn them each day along your journey toward achieving your vision, until these principles become part of your personal habits.

The third and last point for you to focus on in improving your communication is to benchmark yourself and evaluate yourself with the Six Secrets of Communication. How is your communication? Is it too brief? Is it direct? Does it show the impact? Go to the remaining three points and try to restructure your speech, presentation, and communication to fit those Six Secrets of Powerful Communication.

John Powell says, "Communication works for those who work at it."

We will move to the next chapter, which will help us leave a mark and continue our quest to build a legacy.

SOURCES

MindTools.com
http://p4s.pt/en/the-4-pillars-of-emotional-intelligence-and-why-they-matter/
Dale Carnegie, 1998, How to Win Friends and Influence People
Daniel Goleman, 1995, Emotional Intelligence
https://www.rightattitudes.com/2008/10/04/7-38-55-rule-personal-communication/

"Leadership is about making others better as a result of your presence and making sure that impact lasts in your absence."

—Sheryl Sandberg, COO of Facebook

ADD VALUE TO OTHERS

PREFACE

We will be talking about why it is crucial for you to be valuable to others, especially your stakeholders, and how to add value in your presence. What makes you special? We will also cover how to start your first steps toward leaving a significant mark to continue your legacy and your leadership journey.

WHY?

Why do you need to become important to others? Let me share my personal story. In the beginning of my career, I always thought that results were all that mattered to be successful, and it appears that I was wrong. All I ever cared about was meeting the deadline, staying on schedule, being there on time, staying after everybody else left—just doing everything possible to show my dedication and hard work. I targeted all the trophies, all the awards that recognized hard work and commitment, and went the extra mile. Everybody acknowledged my contributions; yet, it wasn't enough. It wasn't the right way because people felt insecure and jealous. I was "succeeding," but I felt alone in the journey. Then it hit me that if I wanted to make an impact, I needed to be social and work with others in order to be recognized and known for my character, skills, and contribution.

I had to build connections with people and impact their way of work. I had to improve communication with others, meaning I had to be part of the team, department or organization I was working with. When you build relationships or connections with others, especially stakeholders, people relate to you more; that helps to build trust and appreciation instead of others being skeptical of you and feeling that your presence and hard work are not helpful to them. In the end, it's not about hard work, results, or numbers; it's the experience, memories, and feelings that you give and share with others that will help you leave a mark and become important. When people see you as a valuable person in the team and in the organization, it is then, and only then, that they will work with you for your success, helping you to become known and perceived as a leader.

HOW?

We will talk about three elements required to make your presence valuable to others.

These are a few tips that I have gathered through my research about this topic:

The first tip is the importance of actively engaging with your team members and colleagues. What do I mean by "actively"? Being interactive means you're being proactive; you're always there when they need you; you are not isolated; you're not living on your own island. With this attitude, your employees, team members, colleagues, and peers will seek out your help and guidance and will be comfortable having you around them. They are more likely to open up to you and trust you, and that will place you in the trust zone of your team members.

The second tip is to always strive to improve and advance in your career, experience, expertise, and skills; this is what I refer to as "The Growth Mindset." Although you may be very good today, there is always room for improvement. You always need to do better because the world is changing; it's becoming competitive, complex, and diverse. Even your competition is changing. You want to be on top of your game. Don't be comfortable in your comfort zone; always push yourself further, seek guidance and feedback, and try to advance your career and yourself no matter what the circumstances.

The third tip is to be knowledgeable and know what is happening around you in your workplace. I'm not just talking about the technical elements; this is more about the political side of the organization and the macro side. That was also another shortcoming I had. I was always only focused on doing my job and completing my task and pleasing my manager, and that was it. I'm not talking about pleasing the manager on a personal level; more so meeting the requirements that the manager or the management requested. That is important, but it's not enough; it misses the big picture. You need to know what is happening around you. For example, if you are working in a corporate environment, you always need to know what's happening in the background. Maybe all of a sudden, a key person who supports you leaves the organization; then your project and work might go to waste. So, you need to be smart, stay aware of what is happening, learn who the major players are and where the major decisions are taking place, figure out what is most important, right here, right now, for this organization, in terms of strategic projects or direction. That way, you can provide the right solutions and useful suggestions, and you will always be aligned with what the management wants, whether you are a consultant or an employee. So, it's not only about hard work and discipline—these are important—but you need to know how to apply them for the right impact.

The fourth tip is don't be negative and focus on other people's mistakes; be positive and save your energy for yourself. Don't care about what others say; don't worry if they did a bad job. We're not here to be judgmental and skeptical. We're not here to compete with them. The best competition to focus on is the one with yourself; so, keep your energy for yourself.

The fifth tip is to be sure to present your ideas positively. In the end, they are your thoughts, and you are the best person to market those ideas. Be focused and powerful in your communication; know what to say, when to say it, and how to say it. Be effective, push your ideas; have the perseverance to get your ideas through. You are the only person that sees them as important, so make sure that your audience sees them as important as well. You need people to take your ideas seriously by finding ways to make them relevant to the stakeholders, over and over again. Put enough emphasis on the points that you want to make in order for people to take you seriously and see things from your perspective.

The sixth tip is to support others' ideas and see how they can apply the ideas better. Many people struggle to share their ideas, and they don't understand how to do it the right way—either publicly or one-on-one. Work with them. Help them. Don't take this as an opportunity to mock them or put them down. Support them, and let them feel that you are a resourceful, caring person. You're not there for the competition. You want to leave an impact by working genuinely with others and letting them know you have a lot to share and give to them.

The seventh tip is to always think about developing work performance and pursuing improvement—any improvement or change, no matter how small. Focus on providing value, not on your image. In other words, focus on bringing value day by day, and show that value. Don't worry about how good or bad you look. In the end, people will see that you are committed to improvement and always enhance performance, and that will be shown in your communication, thoughts, suggestions, and work. Then you will acquire the image that you want for yourself.

The other element that I would like to talk about is included in a great book by Robin Sharma called The Monk Who Sold His Ferrari. It is an inspiring book, and it provides a step-by-step approach on how to live with courage, have balance and abundance, and find joy in our lives. It's one of the top bestsellers in the world. The book talks about a lawyer who worked hard all his life; he had all the money that he wanted and all the titles that he aspired to. He was successful from his point of view, when all of a sudden, he became sick and needed to change the way he thought in order to enjoy what remained of his life.

There are a few words of wisdom that I would like to share in order to help you enjoy life and continue to impact other people's lives.

The first is develop joyful thoughts; have a positive mentality. We talked about the importance of a positive mindset earlier; have love and sympathy for others. This is the first and the most important point.

The second is follow your life's mission and calling. We also talked about this in the section on personal vision and goals. This point will help you find courage, balance, and joy in your life.

The third is to cultivate self-discipline and act courageously. "Be responsible for your life and be disciplined while achieving your goals and milestones in life."

The fourth is to value time as our most important commodity. It's more than time management; it's about valuing every single second of our lives and making the most of our time on this earth. The main takeaway from this point is: don't procrastinate. Just get on with your plans and get moving. We've already wasted a lot of time in our lives doing too many other things that don't have anything to do with our personal vision.

The fifth is nourish your relationships. Help others with no expectation of reciprocity. Don't expect any return from others while helping them. Just do it from the goodness of your heart. Do it because it makes you happy. If anybody helps you back, you'll feel like you're in seventh heaven. You'll be very happy since you do not expect that from them. Value relationships with your family, your siblings, your children, and your coworkers. Any relationship that you appreciate. Build on that, and cherish it as much as you can before you leave that person or things change.

The sixth is to live fully one day at a time; live with gratitude and joy. Have a positive and receptive mindset, acknowledge all the blessings that you have, and enjoy every aspect of your blessed life.

This is the second part on how to leave your mark. The third and last part is discussed in a video I saw by Mark Sanborn. Mark Sanborn is a well-known speaker on leadership; he talks about self-mastery and credibility. In order to have credibility, a person needs to be competent and have the right character and connections or influence. We have already covered competence—it's the ability to deliver as expected. Character is how good you are as a person. Now, after defining your vision and values, what are you planning to do with your life? Every day should make you a better person. Regarding connection and influence, Mark explains that people should want to be like you! That is true and expected from a leader—to be a role model for his or her followers; we talked about that at the very beginning. Our role models are people who we want to relate to and, sometimes, mimic.

I have a personal example of a friend of mine who worked as a tea boy in my previous company; his name is John Matilano. Although John was a tea boy, he always went the extra mile and delivered more than was expected from him. Sometimes, he brought chocolate—he spared his own to offer it to us when he served Turkish coffee; he did not keep it for himself. Every time he brought coffee, the cup was clean; everything was neat. He made sure he delivered five-star service. What amazed me was, all of a sudden, his coffee became even better. I asked him, "Where did you get this coffee from?" He replied, "This is from my aunt from the Philippines. She sent it for me." He shared it with me for three weeks. He shared his aunt's coffee because he is a genuine and caring person who will do what he thinks is the best way to deliver his service. People go the extra mile for what they see as valuable and important. I don't see him as a tea boy. I see that this person can add value to any service industry he may work in. I personally look forward to working with him because I am sure that he will make me look good and successful.

As you see, it's how you perceive yourself. You don't wait for other people to give you credit; you give the credit to yourself and you show people what you're capable of.

Another example of impact and how sincere you need to be can be found in the behavior of Dr. Issa Al-Own, the ex-president of one of the companies I worked for, Triple e Holding. One time, I wanted him to review a communication draft related to department restructuring. He reviewed my draft and corrected it, sharing his comments while doing so. I was impressed because of his depth of knowledge in both Arabic and English, as the communication contained both languages. What shocked me was how he had still maintained his technical writing skills, so I realized I needed to do a better job when coming back to him for future drafts. But what's most important was his genuine interest in helping me to understand why it is crucial to master this skill and how humble he was to teach me. He could have sent me back to my manager for coaching, but he did not. He told me, "Those basic skills we still need to master, no matter how far you go in your job ranking."

These are two examples of leaving an impact that came to my mind in the context of what we are discussing in this chapter.

CONDITIONS FOR SUCCESS

As you can see, there is a lot that can be done to enhance your personal brand and your ability to be valuable to others within your circle. It all depends on how well you utilize these simple steps in your life. So, don't procrastinate. Life doesn't wait for you. Other things will always get in your way, so start with health and family and fulfill your vision.

The next point is don't compare yourself with others. Compare yourself today with yourself yesterday and see how much you have improved. Have you become a better person? Are you closer to your vision? How disciplined are you in achieving your targets and goals compared to a week ago or before reading the book? How committed are you?

Last but not least, no matter how high you go, you still need to know the technical and basic stuff, and you need to do them very well.

LESSONS LEARNED

In this chapter, you have learned simple and practical steps to help you be more effective in living your intentional life. Continue to improve day by day, mentally and professionally. This is important to make you influential, and this can be done by following the mentioned steps on how to be valuable to others. All this will play a big role in making the positive mark that you want to be remembered for.

CALL FOR ACTION

Write a list of ten things that you appreciate in your life every day for the next seven days. Write ten things every day for a week and then see if you can find more. When you think you are done, review the list to realize how blessed you are. Also, practice gratitude as a daily habit. Help someone every day and keep a note of it. Review all the notes on a daily basis, and that will encourage you to continue to help people. This will always keep you fulfilled and help you enjoy your life while being helpful to others and making your mark.

This leads us to the next chapter, which is about leading teams; now you are equipped with all that is necessary to lead yourself and to impact and influence others. In the coming chapter, we will discuss working effectively with teams, whether they are permanent teams or occasional or project teams.

SOURCES

How to Lead Better—video by Mark Sanborn
Robin Sharma, 1999, The Monk Who Sold His Ferrari

CHAPTER 4
AS IN TIMES OF WAR

"Teamwork is the ability to work together toward a common vision. The ability to direct individual accomplishments toward organizational objectives. It is the fuel that allows common people to attain uncommon results."

—Andrew Carnegie

BUILD YOUR TEAM OF WARRIORS

PREFACE

In this chapter, we will discuss the difference between a group and a team, and what it takes to move a group of people to be organized and function as a collaborative team—a team of warriors. Warriors strive for the greater good, and they want to build a legacy for themselves. Such team members follow a visionary leader who motivates and inspires them. We will cover why it is important for these future warriors to join the team, what's in it for them, how to align their visions, what success looks like, and what to consider while building your team using the Action-Centered Leadership Model developed by John Adair in 1973. Then we'll discuss the steps needed to build a successful team and what the different types of teams are.

WHY?

Let's go back to the "Team of Warriors" mentioned in the title! Warriors are aggressive; they are determined to be remembered for their sacrifices, for what they are good at, for their unique character and contributions; they want to be known to future generations as achievers.

Those in a team of warriors put themselves in the line of fire for their beliefs by giving all their energy and engagement, which results in maximum productivity. With full engagement, they can fight their way to victory with their uniqueness, collaboration, and strength. In addition to a team of skillful warriors, the maturity and experience of the team members will help the leader to see the blind spots and ensure the team is moving in the right direction.

What should you consider when building a team? Keep in mind that every team member has his or her own values, styles, interests, and ways of contributing. Team members may come from diverse backgrounds, and belong to different age groups and genders. This is crucial to understanding how they can come together in a team composition.

Michael Jordan, the legendary NBA player, said, "Talent wins games, but teamwork and intelligence win championships." According to Michal Jordan, the keywords are "teamwork" and "intelligence." What does he mean by intelligence? It can be data collection—relevant data and information that improves decision-making and serves the team mission. Talented, smart teammates will help to provide the right suggestions, evaluate the added value of the tasks, and encourage creative thinking. As a leader, you can rely on them as copilots to help ensure that you continue on the right path, achieving and exceeding the desired results.

If you are still in doubt about building a team of strong, talented members, remember that there are twenty-four hours in a day, and seven days in a week. You can't do it alone. Remember, "Two brains are better than one."

Last but not least, always remember to hire people with integrity. Warren Buffett provides a wise, helpful method of identifying the best team member. He said, "We look for three things when we hire people. We look for intelligence, for initiative or energy, and we look for integrity. And if they don't have the latter, the first two will kill you, because if you're going to get someone without integrity, you want them lazy and dumb."

HOW?

I'd like to start with the following quote from Rosalynn Carter, Former First Lady of the United States: "A leader takes people where they want to go. A great leader takes people where they don't necessarily want to go, but ought to be." Here you can see the difference between a leader and an inspiring one. We have already talked about inspiring and influencing others. When you bring the right people on board, you need to inspire them to see their hidden potential and identify opportunities, and the possibilities for achievements, changes, and improvements. This is how team members come together and add value to achieve that dream.

In the beginning, we mentioned that there is a group and there is a team; what's the difference? It is simple. A group can be a weekly or a monthly gathering to read a book or do community service. People come together to do a task but are not fully committed; the gathering is informal in nature, and there's low accountability for members. So, a group is a bunch of people coming together for a purpose. However, there may be no clear vision for the group; it might be simply focused on a short-term purpose. There are no clear roles and responsibilities, no criteria for contribution, no trust involved for the group to come together.

Let us go back to John Adair's model. His Action-Centered Leadership (ACL) Model can be represented by a three-circle diagram that shows that leading teams can be divided into three core elements: what the task is and how to achieve the task; managing the team; and managing individuals.

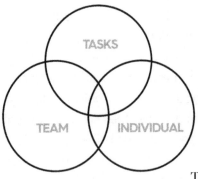

TM: John Adair

Thus, to build a team, you need to identify the task first so that the team has a mission to accomplish. Following task identification, you start to manage the team; everybody has their own responsibility and accountability and an area of contribution based on their expertise, skill set, and individual abilities.

There is another element that is crucial for an effective team to operate according to this ACL: aligning the individuals' values with the team's values for the tasks to be accomplished. These can be either overall team tasks or individual tasks.

As long as we remember to acknowledge and align team members' values within the team and the task, we will be on the right track to achieve the desired results, and maybe more. This is the part that most leaders disregard. In fact, it makes all the difference if you want to bring that magic in building your team of warriors. Remember, passion is derived from values, and values are derived from beliefs that we acquire over decades of our lives, based on our experiences. Make sure your team's values and beliefs are aligned to your advantage. The passion this creates will fuel them to help you achieve your personal vision, personal mission, and what you want to be remembered for.

Let us talk about the task. What do we mean by the task? The "task" is the aim and vision of the group; it is the purpose that gives direction to the team. The type of team does not matter. Is it a project team intended to deliver a certain project and then dissolve or "sunset"? What are the team's goals and objectives? It needs to be specific and measurable. We'll talk more about how to define and measure the team goal to make it accepted by its members and sponsors alike.

You need to undertake the following steps, which are derived from the ACL Model (with some modifications from my end), to form a vision of how the team should perform, and how to ensure we have the right resources for the team to meet and exceed your expectations. I like to call this "the standard of building the team to achieve the desired objectives."

First, you need to check the following:
- Step one: resource identification. You need to define the resources, the people, the processes, the system, the tools—whatever resources are needed to achieve the team's desired goal.
- Step two: you need to create a plan to achieve the goal or task. Finalize the deliverables; define the time scale; explain how you are going to achieve it.
- Step three: establish the responsibilities, what the objectives are and who will be doing what task.
- Step four: set the standards of quality, time, and deliverables.
- Step five: identify what competencies your team will need to accomplish the task; basically, identify what you need and assemble your team based on individual competencies. Determine the size of the team, who will be doing what, how the team will look.
- Step six: Last but not least, describe what's in it for the team members. Acknowledge and invest time to understand why each individual would want to work with you and add value to the team.

This is it in a nutshell—the steps for effective team building: identifying team members, and identifying what is required to achieve that desired goal.

Defining the team's task, vision, or mission will not be the first activity for you. As a leader, you need to decide whether you need a team for a specific task in the first place, or you can do it yourself. Because if you can do it alone comfortably, then why assemble a team? If you need helpers, then it's not a team. A team consists of committed members who contribute, add value, and are accountable and trusted for their deliverables.

These members need to be worthy; they need to have what it takes to be part of that team. They should be inspired by your vision. Once you get their buy-in and they believe in your vision, then your chances of succeeding will double because even if they might not like you, they will still love the outcome. Instead of just being inspired by the leader, everybody will be inspired by that team vision.

The last point I want to highlight is that there are different types of teams. Each team has its own style of involvement, and leaders will vary in how they manage and lead each team. There are two basic types of teams. There is the ongoing team, and there is the improvement or idea generation team. The ongoing one can be a permanent team, which is part of the structure. This team will usually have a leader or a manager who is considered the boss, and the structure will not change unless this person leaves the organization; the team members are there every day. This can be referred to as a normal team in most organizations—a manager and his or her reports. Everybody knows their role, their job description, and their responsibilities—which are fixed. It's very rare that the team members change. In such teams, authority is clear; the delivery and work nature are routine. In these teams, the manager has a high degree of authority since the team style is aligned to delivering predefined, ongoing tasks and the team members come there for a normal work routine. They contribute toward their daily tasks and short-term objectives. Usually, for this type of team to be motivated and to act as warriors, a lot of work is required. That work is usually 30% leadership and 70% follow-up or managing because, in a team of this nature, the team leader's influence is minimal.

The role of such teams is geared more toward compliance than actually raising the bar or challenging the norm. It requires a lot from the leader to convince their manager and sponsors to challenge the status quo and to make a change in the normal work routine. So, it requires a logical, meaningful, objective—which may be more of a quantitative, database type of objective—to show the value for the team members and the stakeholders and to explain why this change is required and why you're pushing for that minor improvement.

The other ongoing team is more like a budget team. In my old company EQUATE, for example, there are ongoing teams, but the members change every year; they have the budget team, the people excellence team, and so on and so forth. These teams deliver the same outcomes every year—for example, controlling the budget. Although the task is different, and the target varies somewhat, the deliverables are essentially the same. For example, one year, the budget committee's goal may be to reduce the budget by 5%, and the next year, the budget reduction might be 10%, but the task of the members will be the same—to reduce the budget to whatever the target is. For this type of team, there will be 50% influencing or leadership and 50% follow-up from the team leader; however, the team leader is different every year, as are the team members. Most likely, they will not be aware of the leadership style, and this leader needs to engage the team members and bring them together to get them motivated. The leader has to help the team members realize their potential within the team by adding value and purpose to what they do; it can reach to 50% impact from the team, and the leader can influence them to deliver better results.

Now, the other type of team is the idea generation or improvement team. This one is usually tasked with developing a new initiative or improvement goal. The team members will challenge the norm. This kind of team can grow from an "intrapreneur" within the organization, a "socialpreneur," such as one in an NGO, or an entrepreneur. For example, when Mark Zuckerberg, cofounder of Facebook, came up with the idea of Facebook, he selected some people and then shared the idea with them, and he created something from scratch. So, this is the type of team that we are referring to as an idea generation team.

In my case, at EQUATE, it was 2018 when I was part of an employee well-being team that was on an organizational level. The team lacked focus and impact, so I took charge of the team, which had representatives of every department and had more than thirty members. The team's focus evolved from corporate wellness to employee wellness; then we ended up with a higher purpose, which was employee happiness. This was a new focus that had never been addressed before, so we created something from scratch; that's what is meant by "intrapreneur." How did I do it? I brought the team members who shared the same values together, and we revisited and redesigned the scope and deliverables. We fine-tuned the team's vision. However, I put the cornerstone in place and defined the big picture; along with the team, we came up with the details along the way.

I want to give another example of an intrapreneur team. In a video of Steve Jobs speaking, he mentions that Apple is the biggest start-up on the planet. So, all the team members at Apple act with an entrepreneur mindset by owning and implementing their ideas within Apple. Employees share their own ideas and lead them from idea creation to implementation. So, this is the mindset that exists in idea or improvement teams. These types of teams require there to be 70% influence from the leader, so the leader's influence needs to be significant, and 30% of effort focused on follow-up or managing the team. Such teams are the ultimate ones. They're more fun and inspiring, although the work is challenging. There is more of a focus on motivation, more of really showing the way to others so that they can make an impact.

To wrap up, keep in mind that for all three different team types, you need to ensure that the personal visions of the individuals are aligned with the team vision and with that of the leader. That way, everybody is fully engaged, productive, inspired, and also empowered to deliver results. Now, if we compare the permanent type of teams to the entrepreneur and intrapreneur type of teams or the improvement teams, we can see there is a big difference among the team types in terms of impact; thus, the permanent team will have the least impact because of the fixed boundaries. However, there is still room to make an impact when we compare one permanent team to another. For example, instead of saving 5%, you can target 10%, and this minor improvement will make a difference. If all departments adapt to this mindset, then your department will be recognized for exceeding performance, which leads to exceptional performance. The mindset to add value will be the new normal for your team. Your team members will be more resilient, more effective compared to other teams and will have the warrior mentality, which will drive success in the projects you lead; the team will be distinguished for the value of its contribution.

The last point to highlight is how to align team goals with team members' interests, or, in other words, consider the element of "What's in it for me?" For those in permanent ongoing teams, this usually relates to how their contribution will be captured through their yearly appraisals or their self-development. Some individuals like to work in teams to learn a new skill or for self-promotion. Maybe it's just for self-interest or exposure. Those are the primary elements; usually a corporate or organizational environment will be an added value or an end result for team members.

For intrapreneur, entrepreneur, and improvement teams, driving change will be satisfying enough as a motivator for the team. They will work with you for the sake of the shared values, passion, purpose, and the goal of changing the norm. Regardless of which type of team it is, people will be inspired to join it. People with altruistic values, for example, will be motivated to work for NGOs such as the Red Cross or the Red Crescent. Others might join such teams for self-development or out of self-interest and also the possible exposure. New graduates seeking internships could also join so they are more likely to be potential hires for the organization.

CONDITIONS FOR SUCCESS

Now we need to identify the conditions that need to be met before we can lead others to success.

First, and most importantly, clarify the team's goal, task, and the desired result, change or outcome.

Second, identify the resources, the processes, and the systems needed to achieve those tasks. You need to ensure that you have the right plan. You probably can share the deliverables and timelines with your mentor or a colleague to make sure that you have a reasonable, practical plan because if the deliverables and the plans are not reasonable or not motivating, your stakeholders, including your team members, may challenge you. Everyone, including the sponsor, your boss, and your team members, needs to have a clear, well-defined plan. This should include responsibilities, quality standards and methods of reporting, the parameters, human resources and others. Don't forget to define what's in it for the team members.

If you're currently leading a team, you might consider the above and evaluate your team alignment on tasks and standards to ensure that the team is heading in the right direction. Your standards will be based on the points mentioned above. You can also consider these standards to improve your leadership and task identification according to the items we've covered. Even if you are not leading a team, you can identify areas of development in your existing one (as a team member) and raise the issue with the team leader. The team's success is your success, and you will be admired for your good observations and team leadership knowledge.

LESSONS LEARNED

Now we have an idea of how to build team vision, objectives, and goals and how to implement the Action-Centered Leadership Model. We know what success looks like, what the possible outcomes and desired states are, how to pay back the team members, and what is required to build a team that will be motivated to achieve great results.

We have understood the following: creating a team vision, and types and examples of team goals; types of teams and how to deal with each situation (the three types of teams); and what motivates others to join your team based on their personal interests, their appraisals, and the opportunities for promotion, exposure, and to drive change.

CALL FOR ACTION

Think of a team you lead or have worked with and reflect on the following questions:

- Of all the teams that you have worked with, in which team were you most engaged and motivated while working?
- What was special about the team?
- How do you think differently about your new team's goals?
- How do you rate the importance of the following leader responsibilities to build a successful team from your point of view?

- Task identification (team and individual tasks and goals).
- Resource identification (people, processes, systems and tools, financials, IT, etc.).
- Plan identification (deliverables, measures, timescales, strategies, and tactics).
- Establish responsibilities (objectives, accountabilities, and measures, by agreement and delegation).
- Set standards (quality, time, and reporting parameters).
- Selection of team members (type of competencies and individuals to accomplish the task).
- Defining what is in it for the team.
- What was a repeated element that usually was weak in your team and the teams that you worked with?
- What do you think was the reason?
- Is that something repeated in your current organization or while you've led a team?

If the same element is being repeated as a weakness within all the teams in the same organization, then this is part of the organizational culture that you need to consider for the future. For example, if "What's in it for me?" was the weak point, then the organization's management needs to be aware of that. If the weaknesses were different in each team, then it's a personal leadership challenge. So, you can highlight that with each leader, if you have a good rapport with them.

If you fall short in resources most of the time, then perhaps you underestimate tasks, fail to negotiate appropriately for resources, or are too confident of delivering the task (ego issue).

Another trap you can fall into is that you may be too considerate in evaluating resources, and you forget about your team members and what motivates them. Or the opposite— you care about motivation and you have the resources, but you lack planning. So, these are the seven elements that you need to go through carefully in order to build your team of warriors!

We discussed how important the team members are, what their competencies are, and how to bring them together as a cohesive team of warriors. The next thing we will cover is how to select the right team members.

SOURCE

John Adair, 1973, Leadership and Motivation

"Getting good players is easy. Getting them to play together is the hard part."

—Casey Stengel

WARRIORS ASSEMBLE

PREFACE

In this chapter, we will discuss the principles of team formation: how to apply the John Adair ACL Model while assembling team members to build a cohesive team, how to build engagement, and how to understand team members' values and contributions. We'll look at the decision-making model in relation to establishing the team norms or code of business conduct, and the necessary tools required to overcome any challenges and problems.

WHY?

Let us go back to the title. What comes to mind? The popular Marvel Avengers. What makes them special is that each member has their unique character, strength, and role within the team. Each hero adds value and contributes to the team, and this is acknowledged and understood. Hawkeye, for example, is an ordinary human being with special skills, who works alongside the Hulk, who has enormous power and strength but none of Hawkeye's skills. Their unique contributions make them important both to the team and to us as viewers. Acknowledging team members' strengths and weaknesses and their characters is vital to establishing the right mixture among team members. For the team to work in harmony and synergy, all members need to know their roles and what makes them special in order to minimize conflict and make it easier for you, as a team leader, to empower them with minimum supervision and follow-up.

Since you are dealing with people, you are dealing with emotions, and emotions play a big role in building trust or conflict. Consequently, you need to clarify the rules of engagement for your team to ensure you lead them to achieve and exceed their goals while keeping team members excited, motivated, and engaged to deliver the highest productivity, creativity levels, and customer experience to clients.

HOW?

Our famous team formation methodology is derived from The Tuckman Team Formation Model. Tuckman breaks down team formation into five steps.

The first step is forming. This is when team members come together. They ask high-level questions; they socialize; they show eagerness, meet each other, and try to understand who else is on the team so they can understand their own role. Above all, they play it safe, seeking to learn the most while taking the fewest risks. This is where the leader's techniques are essential to provide clarity and expectations to the team.

Then we move into storming. This is the challenging stage, where we expect to see resistance, conflict, and, sometimes, competition among the team members; everyone at this point is thinking, "What's in it for me?" Maybe some of them don't participate as they should, either because of their personality or because they are just not sure how to express what they feel and think directly with the team. Some might feel reserved and cautious. This is when the leader needs to encourage the team and explain to the team members the situation and expectations in order for this phase to pass. The storming phase is critical, and if not handled well, you might actually lose some of the team members; it might even break the team altogether if you don't do your homework on team formation well (which was covered in the previous chapter).

Then we move into the norming phase after passing the stressful storming stage. Here, members have worked past their initial conflicts and should be engaged in the team, supporting each other and developing a sense of cohesiveness. The leader at this point should provide feedback and monitoring, since now the team is starting to move forward. And this is where the team defines their code of conduct or rules of engagement for the members.

The next step is performing. Here is where the team gets to show how cohesive and accountable to each other they really are. They will be actually performing. Producing results. Demonstrating their dependence and interdependence on one another. In this stage, there should be minimum intervention from the leader. Here, it's more about encouraging group decision-making and problem solving, and providing opportunities to share information across the team members.

The last step is adjourning; the team performed, they delivered, and now the team is leaving. Usually, people are happy at this point because they have accomplished their goals and they're celebrating. And other team members sometimes feel sad because they recognize that they had good team synergy and have good memories of their time in the group. Here the leader needs to acknowledge the team members for their contributions and acknowledge the impact and the results that they are celebrating.

So, these are five steps of The Tuckman Model.

Under this model, it's particularly critical to navigate smoothly through the storming stage; consequently, it's important to assess and understand the team members' values and strengths. Either we should start off knowing them very well, or we should do a reality check while moving through these stages. In the norming and storming stages, we want to ensure that we have the right team members assembled and that they are motivated and engaged. If they want to be part of the team, it means the team has been well selected, and members should be motivated to work well together. A good exercise, such as a Myers-Briggs personality test, can help determine whether they are engaged or not engaged, whether they are very highly motivated or not as motivated.

I like this test; it's an informal exercise. It will help you iden-tify who's an extrovert and who's an introvert. If you have an extrovert on the team, you should expect them to talk more; if they're not vocally engaged, then there is an issue because it's normally their preference to be outspoken and not think things through thoroughly before they share their ideas. Introverts, in contrast, are more reserved and ana-lytical; you shouldn't expect much talking and discussion from them unless requested. In other words, with the Myers-Briggs test, you can see what to expect from your team members at an early stage.

Another thing to consider while introducing team members is how to explain to the team what each member's unique role is and what the team should expect from them. In some cases, where a member's contribution to the team may be hidden or indirect, you can share the expectation or indirect value with this member. For example, let's say someone is a peacemaker—social, wise, and mature. He or she is a valuable team player, in addition to having exper-tise. You need that person not so much for their technical contribution but for their ability to balance out some of the other team members. This is particularly important if you have some very technical people who might be more judgmental, direct, or stubborn. The peacemaker can bring them together and enable the team to move forward. The leader gets to decide whether and how to share this indi-rect agenda of contributing to the overall value of the team and how to enhance it.

I would like to share a quote by Norman Shidle, the famous author and editor says, "A group becomes a team when each member is sure enough of himself and his contribution to praise the skills of others." This reinforces the importance of everyone understanding why they are valuable—maybe everyone is not equally impactful, but they are all important for the team to achieve growth. This needs to be clarified and agreed to by all members at the outset, not only to acknowledge everyone, but also to make sure they all feel important as well!

Team members can only feel valuable if they are treated as talent, not workers or employees. The difference is that talent has its strengths and challenges. Each team member plays a role that complements and completes team composition. Something else for the leader to consider is individual and team fears, concerns, and doubts. Being aware of people's concerns, whether personal or related to the business or team, helps to shore up and build a teamwork mentality. It better prepares the leader and the team for the challenges that might be ahead so that everyone understands where they're coming from. We expect that people with special characteristics, personality traits, or knowledge will have something to add to the team. This is what we want because we want a team of warriors—people who are willing to move the team by themselves because they have that motivation. They have something valuable to say; as leaders, we need to hear it and acknowledge it.

Then we need to identify and agree on individual responsibilities and objectives for each team member. We need to know who needs to do what and all the parameters for their individual contributions so that they know what to expect from themselves and from others. When everyone knows what to expect, it makes accountability much clearer.

Once the above points have been identified and agreed to by all, it's time to start involving the team. Involve them in all matters; this helps them to feel valued and, consequently, be engaged and motivated. By involving them in problem solving and decision-making, you motivate them to vote for team decisions. Then they will be responsible for their actions because it's their vote, their thoughts, their ideas, and they need to be accountable for them. This will help them remain committed to your success through the team's success and, eventually, their own success as well. This reflects the John Adair model of action-centered leadership, when aligning task, team, and individual goals.

Now, to help with team decision-making and involvement, I will share the model of the Continuum of Shared Decisions. It shows that there are different types of decision sharing the leader can employ. It starts from having all the authority as the leader. The manager or the leader makes the decisions and announces them; sometimes, they permit subordinates or team members to be empowered and function within limits defined by them. This is where what I refer to as high empowerment comes in; that is, empowering the team members. Leadership styles range from acting as the sole authority or micromanaging all the way to an empowerment style in which considerable authority is delegated to members of the team. We can also refer to it as autocratic (boss-centered) leadership and free-rein (subordinate-centered) leadership. You can see in the model the variety of different decision-making and decision-sharing approaches.

From my experience, in the beginning, a leader needs to be firm or autocratic in style. With time and as the team moves through the steps listed above—from forming, to storming, to norming through performing—the leader should move naturally to share increased authority and decision-making with the team members, as they demonstrate their competence and move in the right direction. This builds trust based on the deliverables and the cohesiveness of the team. By the end, the team should have reached a high level of independence and delegated decision-making in alignment with the team's values and guidelines.

All of these approaches can function in different work environments. For example, working in hospital emergency rooms is very different from working in a bank or retail store, which, in turn, is different from working in a start-up. It all depends on the type of environment and team; however, all teams will move through these stages if the team is successful.

CONTINUUM OF SHARED DECISIONS

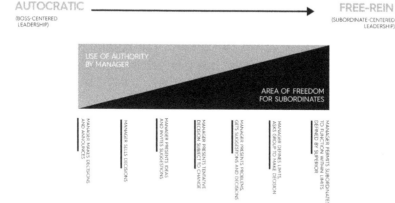

AUTOCRATIC
(BOSS-CENTERED
LEADERSHIP)

FREE-REIN
(SUBORDINATE-CENTERED
LEADERSHIP)

USE OF AUTHORITY
BY MANAGER

AREA OF FREEDOM
FOR SUBORDINATES

MANAGER MAKES DECISIONS AND ANNOUNCES

MANAGER SELLS DECISIONS

MANAGER PRESENTS IDEAS AND INVITES SUGGESTIONS

MANAGER PRESENTS TENTATIVE DECISION SUBJECT TO CHANGE

MANAGER PRESENTS PROBLEMS, GETS SUGGESTIONS AND DECISIONS

MANAGER DEFINES LIMITS, ASKS GROUP TO MAKE DECISION

MANAGER PERMITS SUBORDINATES TO FUNCTION WITHIN LIMITS DEFINED BY SUPERIOR

CONDITIONS FOR SUCCESS

The previously mentioned Tuckman steps will not work if:

- Overall team values, contributions, rules, and responsibilities are not spelled out properly.
- The personalities, the characteristics, and the individual know-how of the team members are not identified.
- The decision-making and team involvement are not clear, and the rules keep changing; for example, one time, you are empowering, the next time, micromanaging, and so on and so forth. This means that the team will get confused and will move into feelings of distrust and a lack of motivation.

What is critical to highlight is the team norms and rules of engagement. This part happens in the norming stage, where team members need to align and agree on norms such as how many times the team will meet, how they will report on team progress, methods of communication, etc. Some refer to team norms as the "team charter." Some refer to them as a "scope of work" and use project management tools. It's up to you how you do it, but every team needs to define their norms. As an example of a team norm: anybody who comes five minutes late to the meeting might be considered absent, and if this continues for three meetings in a row, this person will be ejected from the team. Everybody needs to follow that rule to ensure they are aligned and no one feels neglected or disrespected.

Every leader will be faced with different types of problems. Problem solving is an essential tool for a successful leader. There are six steps for problem solving to overcome team challenges.

- Step one: define the problem.
- Step two: determine the root cause of the problem. There are too many ways of defining the root cause (maybe by using the "five whys" technique) and there is a root causes analysis exercise.
- Step three: once the root cause is determined, then develop alternative solutions.
- Step four: select the proper solution.
- Step five: implement the solution.
- Step six: evaluate the outcome.

As you can see, the approach is straightforward and very helpful in dealing with the problems faced with the team. Of course, when we say "a problem," it most likely affects more than one team member. If the problem is related to one team member, then the team leader needs to take them aside and deal with it one-on-one, but it can also be applied to one-on-one coaching. If we don't follow a proper approach for problem solving, then we will be making assumptions and jumping to conclusions, which is a mistake. People think that they know, so they judge, and this is what most people do: judge others. Always take your time, play your full role as a leader, be the role model, and go by the book. By doing this, you will ensure that your team has full synergy and the right team spirit to deliver the results.

LESSONS LEARNED

In this chapter, I have explained The Tuckman Model of team development, mainly the forming, storming, and norming stages, and how to lead the team effectively through these three phases. In the next chapter, we'll talk about the performing and the adjourning.

We have covered how to build the team's vision and individual visions—team vision based on the individuals' visions and alignment of the tasks. If team members do not want to be there, that means either they are not aware of the value that they have for the team, or maybe the wrong team members have been selected.

We discussed how to acknowledge personal values, personality types and characteristics, and looked at individual contributions and knowledge. We covered decision-making techniques and tips for increasing involvement. We also looked at how important it is to establish team norms, rules of engagement and problem-solving steps in order to ensure that we move from forming to storming to norming and, from there, to performing.

CALL FOR ACTION

Prepare ahead of time to inspire and lead the team to get the best performance through engaging everyone's heart and mind. This can take place by considering the correct match between the task and the individual in terms of interest and capability so that the individual can clearly see the payoff and that the greater good for the team will benefit them as well. In other words, the more the end result and the tasks are clear and achievable, the more motivated the team members will be. No matter how challenging the task to be achieved is, the team will do their best to get it done. The greater the impact of the team, the more team members will act like warriors and push themselves to succeed.

The next step is to explore how individual contribution works, how to set clear measured tasks and develop actions and accountabilities, and how to build trust by having open communication with team members in order to lead the team effectively.

SOURCES

https://navidmoazzez.com/best-personal-branding-quotes/
https://www.forbes.com/sites/josephliu/2018/04/30/personal-brand-work/#6d0cd31b7232

"A leader must inspire or his team will expire."

—Oren Woodward

CHOOSE YOUR BATTLES

PREFACE

W e will explore the essence of effective teamwork and what is required to achieve team goals. We will go through a set of standards to set smart goals for individual members to deliver as expected. We'll explore team communication between the leader and the team and among team members, what we can do to build and enhance trust within the team, and how to build clear accountability for team members and the leader.

WHY?

Let's go back to the title "Choose Your Battles." We will look at this concept by using inputs from The Carrot Principle, a book that explains how to motivate team members to achieve their goals by correctly defining the following four elements: (i) setting the right goals, (ii) establishing a means of communication, (iii) building and enhancing trust, and (iv) maintaining accountability. These elements help us monitor the team's performance and ensure team cohesiveness and motivation. In this way, we can ensure that no one feels they are overwhelmed or are a victim in any way. The leader and the team together should agree on deliverables and set goals that are measurable and achievable. Then the communication standards to share feedback, results, updates and learning must be set, in addition to team norms and rules of engagement. To build trust within the team, it is essential to involve and engage the members by having open discussions and collaboration while establishing the team standards. If this is done, but there is no trust or we do not give enough focus to trust-building, then everyone will simply act for himself or herself. And that means that there is no team because that's not teamwork anymore.

According to The Tuckman Model, as we move from the norming stage to performing, trust needs to be continuously developed to reach the adjourning stage successfully.

Trust needs to be monitored and modeled by the leader, who needs to encourage teamwork. In addition, the leader needs to ensure accountability. With clear accountability, expectations, and ownership, the team will perform well. If accountabilities are not clear and there's a lack of ownership, then no one will deliver their part and the team will fail. Even if there is trust, clear goals and communication, but the team is not delivering as per the agreed standards, then what is the point? The team is still failing. This means that the team members are not taking the job seriously, and the team's tasks are not in their lists of priorities.

HOW?

A good way to start the process of goal setting, especially since most people work in organizations or as entrepreneurs, is to follow a Management by Objective Goal Setting approach. Peter Drucker, one of the founding fathers of management, developed this concept. Management by Objective cascades the strategic-level objectives of the organization to the managers and team members, so all objectives are fully aligned and serve the overall strategy.

Professor Robert S. Rubin from St. Louis University produced further work in this area and came out with the SMART objectives. SMART is an acronym for a different set of characteristics to establish an objective goal. So, to learn how to make our goals for the individuals and also the top main goal of the team clear and reachable, we will explore the SMART objectives one by one.

S stands for specific. Is the goal or objective specific and clearly identified for all stakeholders? Is it simple, sensible, and significant?

M stands for measurable. Can we quantify it? Others would add, is it meaningful and motivating? This is my favorite addition.

A is for achievable. Can the goal actually be achieved or attained?

R is for relevant or relevance. Is the goal relevant to the role, to personal values, to personal interest, or personal and career aspirations? Maybe you work in the IT sector and there is a role, activity or task related to finance; if you have an aspiration to move to finance, then this would be a relevant activity. Another example: you work in a team related to sales and marketing, but your goal is to build business knowledge, then sales and marketing experience is also relevant. So "relevant" is not only related to your direct job role. Relevance needs to be there. We can also use R for reasonable and realistic. Reasonable in this sense can be replaced with attainable; for example, you cannot ask for 90% customer satisfaction if you know it's impossible to achieve based on your relevant data. We can validate a reasonable and realistic goal by asking the following: Do we have the right resources to achieve the goal? Is it result-based?

T stands for time-bound. Is the goal time-based? Is there is a time limit for it? Can it be done in a timely manner?

So, a SMART goal is specific, measurable, achievable, relevant, and time-bound; this is a well-defined objective to review and update, which applies to team and individual performance evaluation.

I prefer a slight variation on the SMART objectives: significant, motivating, achievable, result-oriented, and time-bound. I believe this is motivating, and I recommend that you adapt the objectives in the same way because starting with significant will provide more impact than starting with specific. So, significant and motivating show that it's worth the effort—especially as there is a hidden rule about goal setting, namely that it needs to be challenging. Why?

Because if you have the same resources and you keep delivering the same results every year, then it means that you are not growing. You need to show your worth and that you are growing in your expertise, skills, maturity, and experience level; you are expected to take on challenging roles and tasks. Challenging goals are expected, but do not overstretch yourself and your team in a way that means the goals cannot be achieved; they need to fit into those five elements. Otherwise, we're just wasting our time, and the team members will be demotivated.

As mentioned, SMART objectives are applied at all levels. Although they are agreed upon and clear, the goals always need to be reviewed and reassessed to adjust the plans, methods, and targets as necessary. This doesn't have to be done every day or every week, but it should be done at least every quarter or every six months based on the management or sponsor's decision, or maybe in response to external changes and circumstances. Then, of course, the team needs to be informed of any changes.

Now let us go deep into each of the four elements, starting with accountability. So, what are the steps of accountability that need to be practiced by leaders to ensure clear communication with team members?
- Set a standard on reporting on progress for the individual and the team.
- Anticipate and resolve group conflicts.
- Establish and agree on communication standards of performance and behavior.

- Enable, facilitate, and ensure effective internal and external group communication.
- Identify and meet group-training needs.
- Give feedback to the group on overall progress; consult and provide feedback from and to the group.
- Give recognition and praise to individuals and the team; acknowledge good work, and reward individuals with additional responsibilities and advancement.

These communication and accountability standards were derived from the ACL managerial tasks or leadership tasks.

Now that you are exposed to accountability standards, decision-making and problem-solving methods, you are equipped with what you need to overcome challenging situations with your team. Yet, we also need to acknowledge and overcome team conflict.

We always need to anticipate this and be ready to resolve conflict quickly and appropriately. Conflict is different from disagreement; it is more complex. If left unsolved, conflict can damage the team morale and trust.

Let us explore a conflict management method that I personally use and deliver in my training on resolving conflict. It is a five-step method, which can be explained as follows:

- Step one is to acknowledge the conflict and agree to solve it. When you have a conflict with a member, you both need to acknowledge that there is one. You cannot move forward unless it is resolved; if the conflict is between the leader and team member, or between team members, the leader needs to step in to understand the situation.

- Step two is to understand the situation and gather the facts—all the facts, both qualitative and quantitative, all the input, everyone's thoughts on what happened and how the problem occurred.

- Step three is to verify and analyze data. Make sure you have the correct information to help you in making the right decision. Sometimes, you can refer to the root cause analysis or the "five whys"; although it's a problem-solving technique, it can be used for conflict resolution.

- Step four is to think "win-win" to reach an agreement. Win-win basically means both parties will sacrifice. When we say "sacrifice," we mean a sacrifice that is made to reach a compromise. This means that we don't lose all our rights and the things that we demand from the other person because if we do that, it will be a lose-win, and the other person will take everything that they requested. When we say "win-win," it means I give up some of the things that I want and keep the most important things, and the other person does the same. So, for example, suppose I want to use some of the resources of the team or additional team members to complete my task as an individual in the team. This means, I might disrupt the team, but I see it as important for the overall benefit of the team, even if the other team members disagree. Then win-win will be that we can reach an agreement that I can use additional team members for one month to complete the task instead of my original request of three months' time. This will maintain trust while achieving what needs to be done for the team, without creating additional conflict.

- Step five is to do what you can to prevent future conflict.

These are the five steps of the conflict management method, and now we go for building trust. So, what are the steps that the leader needs to do to build trust, boost trust, and gain the trust of the team members?

- Assist and support individuals. Mentor, support, and guide your team. If any member faces certain problems in delivery or even on the personal level, the leader needs to be there to support them and ask team members to support them as well.
- Respond immediately to team members; you need to be available for your team. If you set this example, other team members will do the same and will provide support to other team members, which will boost trust within the team.
- Train and develop your teams. This can also be considered as trust-building because the team will feel that you care about them and want them to succeed.
- Develop individual freedom and authority.
- Introduce team members to key stakeholders. Let them see that they will earn exposure, and there is nothing you are hiding from them. They will see that you are giving them the opportunity to be known and are sharing

the success with them, not standing on their shoulders or taking the credit on their behalf.
- Last but not least, provide access to relevant information or databases. It is important for them to gain information and to know that there is nothing you are hiding from them; so, it is very important.

The last and fourth step is to ensure accountability. We can achieve this by doing the following:
- Control and maintain activities within agreed parameters.
- Monitor the overall performance against the agreed deliverables and targets.
- Monitor and maintain discipline and integrity and help the team focus on objectives.
- Assess and change when necessary. A leader might need to change the team composition or team members; maybe they will need to readjust activities if accountability is not going in the right direction.
- Develop the collective maturity and capability of the group by increasing group freedom and authority, as illustrated in the decision-making diagram of a continuum of shared decisions. So, as you develop trust with the team members and they start to deliver, you can share more actions with them, and this will also contribute to building trust.

There is no black and white here; it's just a matter of making things more relevant and helping us do what is required to ensure the team is performing and moving in the right direction.

CONDITIONS FOR SUCCESS

Now for this to work, you as a leader have to establish clear values and goals and must discuss the issues facing the team, whether they are internal or external matters. Share them with the team so there is full transparency. Keep the team updated and informed. Always make time for individuals. Always keep open communication lines; as already mentioned, respond immediately to team members. You need to do this whether or not you're leading teams. Admit your errors and mistakes in public. Always keep your word and follow through on your promises. Surround yourself with people who you trust, who demonstrate honesty, and who have experience. Do not participate in matters of suspicion, doubt, or deception. Actively contribute to building a positive reputation for yourself, your team, and your organization.

LESSONS LEARNED

In this chapter, we have covered what it takes for the team to perform in the right way by establishing goals objectively, understanding how to be clear and measurable and observable by others, setting clear communication protocols, and enhancing trust among team members. Finally, you need to establish accountability measures to ensure that you get the results that have been agreed upon. We also discussed conflict management steps that will enable you to be fully equipped to get the results that you want and to overcome conflicts within the team.

CALL FOR ACTION

Reflect on the four steps of The Carrot Principles: (i) set goals, (ii) establish communication, (iii) build trust, and (iv) establish accountability. Think of the worst team you worked with. What elements of the four were missing? Now think about the best team you encountered; how did they do with the four elements? Consider why the worst team was missing one or more elements, and why the best team had the majority or all of the elements covered. Also ask yourself, what would you do differently for the current team you are leading, or for future teams, to ensure your team will perform as you have planned or even better?

Now we have moved to the performing stage and understanding what is needed to build the right team—assembling the right members with the right qualities, characteristics, and

knowledge—and the correct way to encourage engagement and motivate the team to perform. In the next part,
we will discuss what it takes to keep the team motivated to
continue delivering exceptional results.

SOURCE

https://www.mindtools.com/pages/article/smart-goals.htm

CHAPTER 5
PULL THE TRIGGER

"People work for money but go the extra mile for recognition, praise, and rewards."

—Dale Carnegie

WHERE TO START?

PREFACE

We will dive deep into the theories of motivation formulated by the world's renowned leaders of motivation and explore how we can ensure that we have the right balance between external and internal motivators.

WHY?

"You can lead a horse to water, but you can't make it drink." What we are referring to is the fact that, as leaders, sometimes you keep doing all you can to motivate your team members or other individuals to help themselves. Now, most, if not all, of us have gone through the same with a family member, colleague, a peer, or someone we care about. Perhaps you tried to show them the way, but they were just not interested because they did not see the need or the why! They would rather just feel sad for a little while; they don't see the long-term effect or the big picture of how they need to help themselves to do something to change their lives. We know that most people like to be in their comfort zone. Unfortunately, there is no greatness in remaining in your comfort zone, but what can you do about this?

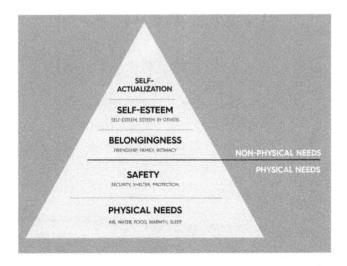

As a leader who wants to prevail, you need to enhance your ability and understand the psychology of motivating others. Where to start? Maybe you are familiar with Maslow's Hierarchy of Needs. It's a very well-known framework, and the first level refers to the very basic needs, which include essential survival needs: air, water, food, warmth, and sleep.

The second level is seeking a feeling of safety. Once the survival needs are met, then a person would seek security, shelter, and protection; these are the basic physical needs.

The third level includes the non-physical needs: a sense of belonging, affection, acceptance, and being loved.

The fourth level is esteem, including self-esteem and appreciation by others. The fifth and last step is self-actualization. So, if someone lacks the basic or physical needs, don't expect them to go for self-actualization. What it means is that someone has all they need to cover their basic physical needs—they have a home, they have a family, they have a good job and good income—but they want to take it to the next level. They want to inspire others. They want to do more, like Elon Musk, for example. He has enough money to meet his physical needs; yet, still, it's not enough—he wants to leave his mark, his legacy. This is the goal we started with; the book is intended to help you start your legacy based on your personal vision.

It has been said that the more employees are involved in decision-making that affects their work, the more engaged and supportive they will be. This is especially true in organizations where office employees with white-collar jobs aim for the self-esteem and self-actualization levels. It's important for them to be recognized and feel valued, so involving and sharing decisions is highly motivating for them.

Getting them motivated in those two or three categories of non-physical needs will take a lot of work. And it is very critical that we understand how Maslow's pyramid of needs is reflected in the workplace, whether it is a private

organization, publicly shared business, or even an NGO—
basically, in any type of organization.

HOW?

John Adair says, "A want is a need that is conscious."
Basically, when someone wants something, they are aware
of the importance of that thing. Now, whether it's legitimate
or not, whether it's right or not, is not the point. Let us take
the example of someone who wants a fancy car. That
person feels that this acquisition is very important based
on their need or perception. However, what we want to
learn is how to make our team members feel a need to
be engaged and deliver the results that they should be
delivering.

My golden rule is that in order to inspire and motivate
others, focus on changing their mindset by helping them
realize what is a need and what is a want. After this, the
want will become the drive. When people acknowledge
the need to do something—for example, being part of
your team—once they see the value of the activity and
understand what's in it for them, then they will want to
join the team and contribute to the overall goal. Now their
want will be the driver and motivation to achieve their
goals and the team goal.

As we explained, Maslow's Hierarchy of Needs is reflected
in most office environments. We can safely say that a

majority of white-collar workers who are potential stake-holders and colleagues are at the third or fourth level of Maslow's hierarchy; perhaps some of them are even in the fifth stage of self-actualization. For example, now that the coronavirus has impacted societies around the world, people all of a sudden have lost their jobs, particularly entry-level and senior positions in organizations; many of them have to work for half of what they were paid earlier or for free! As you can see, you can drop from self-actualization to level three. If the needs of the levels are not met, then the motivators will change for each individual based on their situation. For example, someone who is a manager would normally be safe, but they might unexpectedly find their job threatened by circumstances beyond their control. So, here, this person actually is moving to stage number two. And that affects their concentration and their productivity; don't expect this person to think clearly and push your team to achieve exceptional results. That is why you have to be close to your team, so that you can understand their personal circumstances.

However, this should not prevent you, as an aspiring leader, to inspire and motivate your team. According to John Adair's 50/50 Rule, you can do it. So what is this rule?

It states that there are two factors contributing to peoples' motivation. The first 50% depends on the person or is within the person; this can be described as the internal factor. The other 50% is the external factor, which includes the manager, the environment, monetary and non-monetary conditions affecting the person, and so forth. If a person is already self-motivated, then your job as a leader is 50% done!

Since we are taking Maslow's pyramid as our framework, we can expect that the higher the level a person is at, the more they should be satisfied and eager to move to the next level.

Back to the external 50%—this is mostly related to the leader because the leader is responsible for creating and directing the workplace environment. It's said that a good environment is why people join companies, and 75% leave because of poor managers!

So, as a leader, you can impact and you can influence and you can improve 50% of your employees' or team members' motivation. The other 50% needs to be changed from within.

Looking at Maslow's hierarchy through a corporate lens, it can be applied to an employee's engagement perspective, according to an employee's rank.

Remember that the first level is survival. Employees at this level are going to be disengaged. They are just waiting for their paycheck at the end of the month; they want to comply with the system to receive their compensation. They're just there to survive, and they are not willing to challenge the norm or even care to inspire others. They just hope that they remain healthy and can come to work every single day to earn their money. Expect minimum productivity and no creativity from people at this level; basically, they are in it for the cash.

Employees at the next level make better ones. They are productive, but they're still disengaged. Maybe they're known for frequently taking sick leave. Maybe they experience problems with their direct managers. They might not be getting along with their supervisors and are usually actively seeking to join other teams, departments, or even employers. Maybe it is just simply that they are not engaged. These first two levels include a lot of the negative emotions and demotivated groups; these employees are not going to be motivated.

Continuing to the third level—here, the people are more productive and more likely to feel that they are part of the vision of the organization or the team. They are somewhat proud and sometimes engaged. They do not believe in career progression; they are more practical and less aspirational.

People at the fourth level are the achievers. They usually are more stressed because they feel they are important and adding value to the team and organization. However, if they find something better, they wouldn't mind transferring or relocating; they're happy to take better opportunities or a better role within the organization, or even outside of the organization or the team. You should find most of your team members and supporters within the achievers.

The self-actualization level is where employees are very committed and highly engaged; they come to work for pleasure rather than just because it's their job. They see their work as a passion, and they seek to inspire and help others. Usually, you see them in the role of mentors; they are well-respected within the organization and the team.

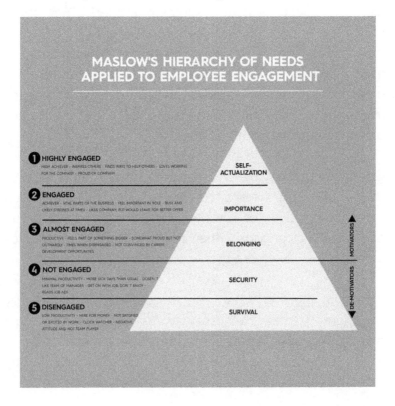

INDIVIDUAL WELL-BEING
(MASLOW'S HIERARCHY OF NEEDS)

SELF-ACTUALIZATION
MEANING, PURPOSE, MORALITY, CREATIVITY, SPONTANEITY, PROBLEM SOLVING

SELF-ESTEEM
CONFIDENCE, ACHIEVEMENT, MUTUAL RESPECT, UNIQUENESS

LOVE AND BELONGING
FRIENDSHIP, FAMILY, INTIMACY

SAFETY AND SECURITY
RESOURCES, PROPERTY, EMPOYMENT,
HEALTH, SOCIAL STABILITY

PHYSIOLOGICAL NEEDS
BREATHING, FOOD, WATER
SEX, SLEEP,
HOMEOSTASIS,
EXCRETION

As you can see, Maslow's law covers the 50% of internal factors that explain the needs and the wants of an individual according to their position in the five levels. This is helpful to identify the triggers of each employee, and where to find the right pool of talent based on your team objectives.

We have a very useful theory to cover the external element of motivation from the very well-known Frederick Herzberg and his Theory of Motivation, which can be explained in two parts:

Motivating factors cover the factors that make the person do the additional work or go the extra mile.

Hygiene factors are the factors that hinder and minimize employee motivation if they are not done well.

So, what do the hygiene factors consist of? They include the following:

- Direct manager or the leader.
- Work conditions, job location, office location, office setup, etc.
- Salary and benefits.
- Policies and systems.

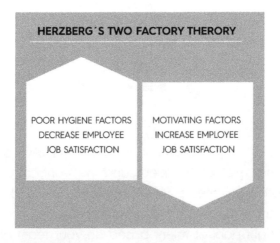

You may have noticed that all these factors are related to the organization's policies, culture, and environment; they are not related to the job or the role of the person. Thus, the same work conditions applied to the leader are applied to others, including current and future team members.

Now let us explore the motivators, which could include recognition of the type of work itself (can be more strategic versus operational), the nature of the work (more office-based than manual labor, for example), advancement, promotion, development, recognition, and so on and so forth. These factors are related to the job itself. With this, we have covered both internal and external factors that impact personal motivation for employees.

As you can see, the motivators partly fall under the influence of the team leader or the manager. However, the maximum you can impact as a leader is 50%. So, you cannot push yourself too much because the remaining 50% is out of your control. What needs to be highlighted is the fact that external factors can be out of the organization's control. Such factors may be related to a person's residency, family, and other conditions, which are considered part of physical needs. Thus, in order to relate to your team members and help them, you need to truly understand where they fit within Maslow's hierarchy and Herzberg's hygiene factors, and what problems or challenges they are facing.

In order to motivate others, you need to make sure that you have everything clarified. When you pick the right people, they need to be placed in positions where they can contribute significantly, even if they are focused on physical needs. This is because the opportunity that you are giving them should include the aim of helping them move up the ladder into the next level (belonging), while others may aim to reach the self-actualization level.

Here, I'd like to share the story of the movie Patch Adams. Robin Williams acted in the role of the doctor who was very creative in his bedside manner. Most of his colleagues didn't understand the value of creativity or understand his motivation to really make his patients feel better and happier. He went through tough times. He was very clear on what he wanted—to reach the self-actualization level. Even though he dropped down to the safety level—Maslow's second stage— he managed at the end to be well-known and successful, reaching self-actualization by doing what he wanted and being successful and known for it. Another example of self-motivation is a guy who should be at the physical needs level; he is low on both the hygiene factors and in Maslow's pyramid, but he travels the world to inspire others. Nick Vujicic was born without arms and legs; yet, he is successful and famous for his motivational speaking business!

CONDITIONS FOR SUCCESS

To succeed, you must ensure that your team's basic needs are met. In order for you to have an exceptional team that produces exceptional results, they need to have both their physical and hygiene needs met. Otherwise, you should reconsider the impact or the change that you will create working in the current environment, whether it's with a current organization as a whole or with individual team members.

If you want to have a great impact and you're working in an organization where the team members do not feel secure, and they're basically in survival mode or disengaged or even below the belonging mode, then don't expect much from that organization. No matter how great your impact, your ability to succeed is going to be minimal compared to working in an organization where most of the people are at the esteem and self-actualizations levels. Here is where the magic happens, and this is why most people in big and successful organizations succeed in life—because they have all the basic needs, and they are ready to go the extra mile to take risks, be creative, and change the world.

You don't need to be in a world-leading organization to achieve this; we are not asking that you work for Google or Apple. There are good, well-known organizations in the Middle East and North Africa regions that have so much potential; some are world leaders, such as Aramco and SABIC. Work in an environment that helps you achieve your self-actualization goals and make the impact that you want.

LESSONS LEARNED

We have introduced two of the main motivational theories globally recognized in human motivation and the needs related to the individual according to each theory.

We have covered the 50/50 Rule to help you engage your team, identified the areas of your influence, and defined what you can influence and what you need to take care of while leading other people. We've covered how to identify the right pool, pick the right people, and how this applies to the corporate environment.

CALL FOR ACTION

As a leader, you need to identify where you fall on Maslow's Hierarchy of Needs. What you need to do is reach up to the self-actualization level because if you want to lead with impact and leave a legacy, you need to be operating with your best self, resources, and team members in order to leave that mark and achieve your vision.

If you are not at the self-actualization stage, then look at what hygiene factors may be negatively affecting you. If it is the workplace or the environment that you're working in, then you need to change that environment.

Then move to the motivators and evaluate if you are getting enough of these motivators, and identify how to get more of them. You need to keep pushing yourself forward, whether you get those motivators or not, because now you are self-motivated. You need to be self-motivated in order to achieve your vision because this is your passion; this is how you want to be remembered; and this is how you prefer to live your life.

These three steps are crucial in order to get the benefit of the knowledge provided about motivation.

Next, you will be provided with tools to help you motivate your team based on the motivational theories and models discussed earlier. These tools will enable your team to achieve their greatness and you to achieve yours.

SOURCES

https://www.researchgate.net/figure/Maslows-hierarchy-of-human-needs_fig4_269702719
https://www.patheos.com/blogs/sacrednaturalism/2017/10/an-evolutionary-hierarchy-of-needs/
http://www.nextlevelbd.co.uk/2018/08/06/1325/
https://expertprogrammanagement.com/2018/04/herzbergs-two-factor-theory/

"Nothing great was ever achieved without enthusiasm."

—Ralph Waldo Emerson

TEAM OF UNSTOPPABLES

PREFACE

To focus on how to maintain our integrity, we will discuss the difference between motivation and manipulation. Then we will understand how to motivate ourselves, what the best ways to identify highly motivated people are, how to determine the right rewards for the team and individuals, and how to treat team members as people and individuals instead of as employees.

WHY?

In the book The Carrot Principle, author Chester Elton states, "If we reward the team members, then we can be trusted because we are rewarding the right behavior." Plus when you recognize your team members, they will trust you more because they will see that you don't take credit for their work. As long as they're being recognized within the team, especially in public or in front of stakeholders for their team and individual contributions, you will be reinforcing and encouraging the desired behavior and actions. By implementing the right motivation tools such as reward, recognition, appreciation, and so on and so forth, in the right way, you can exert a very powerful impact to enhance trust among the team members and deliver more productivity, engagement, and exceptional results.

Chester Elton says, "Power of recognition will lead your team to new levels of achievements." As per management books, theories, and data analysis on what is the number one motivator of employees and teams, usually it's not the money; in fact, money isn't even among the top three or the top five motivators—it is maybe the seventh or ninth one. However, this applies to the higher levels and employees who have options to find another job, although they may attract less in benefits. Remember when people work in organizations or teams, they usually would have already met their physical needs. Money will come anyway, if you follow the process of achieving your vision. When the team feels they are contributing and showing their strength and being acknowledged for their unique value, they are more satisfied. The entry-level employees do care more about compensation. But many, especially those aspiring to self-actualization, do not care about the money; they care about recognition. The environment and culture are shaped by leaders and reflect leaders' behaviors. That's why management style plays a significant role in employee retention; it is the management that shapes the engagement and productivity that drives employee satisfaction.

What I am emphasizing is that recognition is the fuel! This is the fuel that we are going to use to ensure that our team is achieving its targets and tasks, maintaining ongoing communication, and enhancing their trust and accountability while working in the team.

HOW?

I mentioned that there is a difference between manipulation and motivation; so how can we define manipulation? Manipulation is fake; it's not based on truth.

It is used for the benefit of one person over the other person; it is win-lose. Yet, the person might not realize that others have taken advantage of them by lying and deceiving. In many cases, manipulators are leaders or managers. They may use the data and facts for their personal benefit over that of their reports or team; this is unfair, immoral, and not accepted by any culture's ethical framework. It's definitely a very poor leadership behavior. Manipulation is fake and selfish; it is a tactic of the weak and the greedy. It's about controlling other people, and will result in mistrust among team members; this will lead them to disengage from the process and destroy the leadership brand. However, motivation is genuine; it is real. Motivators think of the benefit to others or the team members over their personal benefit. It's encouraging, supportive and empowering.

With that being said, let's explore how to start the motivation process.

First, as a leader, you need to motivate yourself. Yes, yourself! Because you are human, you have needs, wants, and drives. No one said that you are an angel or have superpowers. You're a person with a vision—a person who has demonstrated that you have the credibility, discipline, courage, and humility to reach where you are today. Even if you think that you don't have all of that for now, you should seriously consider those values, along with integrity, as you move forward to achieve your vision and live passionately. You have your own problems and challenges, and you need to motivate yourself. As you are the leader, you have a vision for the team, and you push everyone toward that vision. You realize its impact, and it means more to you than anyone else.

As Rhyanna Watson, the famous health & wellbeing consultant says, "Push yourself because no one else is going to do it for you." You need to motivate yourself and be persistent. You're on your own with this one, so how can you do it? A good way to start is to identify highly motivated people, be around them, and adopt their way of thinking. This will help you in motivating yourself and your team. Also make sure that you invest a lot of time in motivating your team on a personal and team level; that's very critical.

An important note here: make sure you differentiate team members who truly are motivated to add value versus the ones who only act like they care. You could encounter some people who might fake motivation and excitement to join your team out of some personal interest, but these people might not really engage with the team or concern themselves about the team's success. You need to be very careful to not select these types of people as team members.

Treat team members as people, not as employees. What does that mean? Treat them as talent and as individuals. Even the term "Human Resources" is becoming outdated and alternative terms are being used such as "Talent Management," "Human Capital," or just "People"; there are companies who employ someone with the title of "Chief People Officer"! So how does this emerging philosophy differ from the one found in the traditional model of HR or employees? In the previous model of HR, only 5% to 10% of employees were considered talent—high flyers or high-potential employees or star performers—while the rest were just considered employees, largely interchangeable and disposable. In modern HR and management practices, we consider every person as a talent because every person in this world is unique; everyone has unique character, strengths, and contributions to make. Everybody has their identity and background. This is why we see a lot of the phrase "diversity in the workplace," where companies seek to build more value in their workforce through a more diverse pool of manpower. So, you need to deal with each member as talent; everyone has their own needs, their own life, and their own wants and needs. Consider all that when dealing with people—your people, your talents.

Also focus on leading, not managing. We haven't talked much about management here; our focus has been on leadership. Like Peter Drucker always says, and this is one of the mottos I use in life when leading others: "Managers do things right." So, they do things in the correct manner as per the book and as per the policies and procedures, while "Leaders do the right things!" So, a leader would overrule the procedure. They will take a risk where they see that overriding a company policy is for the greater good. If the situation requires an exception, if it will work best for the team and the organization in the long run, then they will do what is required to make this right. This is the role of a good leader. Don't break all the rules, but if you do break one, make it for the sake of your team and for the sake of others. In the end, it should benefit the organization. Being a leader will give you confidence and will make you feel good about yourself and give you the right dose of motivation to move forward.

Then, to be happy and motivated while you're delivering the work, set realistic and challenging goals. Why realistic? So the goals can be achieved. Why challenging? To make you feel excited to achieve the goals. This will help you build new skills and stretch yourself in a positive way; when the goals are achieved, it will boost your confidence.

Keep a calendar and mark every milestone of your projects and life plan; then celebrate along with the team members or even on your own, as long as you identify what type of reward you will give yourself for leading yourself or leading the team to an accomplishment. You deserve it. Don't overlook small accomplishments, either; remember that every bit of progress serves to motivate you.

Let us discuss rewards as incentives to motivate people. Rewards can be for different things and usually are tangible; they should be given for achievement above and beyond the norm. Keep rewarding people in line with these principles, but always try to make sure rewards for objective actions aren't vague or subjective. If they seem arbitrary, it might affect people's trust and make other people feel things are not fair. Make sure that from the beginning, while you're defining the team norms, you are explicit about what is considered above and beyond normal achievement levels and what rewards exist for team members who manage this level of performance. You don't have to agree with it 100%, but at least it needs to be fair enough for all to serve its purpose and not to backfire against your leadership style.

You also need to know both what should be rewarded and who should be rewarded. Usually, rewards are earned for modeling desired behavior as described in team norms; this can be teamwork, creativity, quality of work, accuracy of work, saving time—there are many more examples of being a team player and enhancing team spirit. For example, a team member may have had challenges coping with coworkers and improved his or her behavior to work well with the team. Or a team member may have been a mentor to the team and helped the members to develop their skills.

Rewards can be presented by the leader to the team, or by the team to team members, or maybe even by the team to the leader.

In terms of above-and-beyond achievements, the reward can be delivered to someone who went the extra mile to exceed the expected results, challenged hindering external circumstances, and managed to deliver as expected. It could be someone who delivered with less resources or delivered more value than expected. It all depends on the task.

So, what are the types of rewards you should use? Well, usually, rewards come in two forms: tangible or intangible. Rewards can be very simple gifts, such as a cake or a note. They can be given on a weekly basis to different team members. They can be something like an informal lunch, or ordering pizza for the team even without an occasion. It can be on the spot, spontaneous, and on the go, to enhance team spirit. You can celebrate anniversaries or invite team members to attend random celebrations. If you're giving rewards, make them frequent. Keep costs low, but make sure they have a high-end touch.

We discussed The Myers-Briggs personality test and other activities that help you know your team on a personal level. It can help you know each person's likes and dislikes, their hobbies, what really makes them happy, what they like to have, what they want to be, and many more factors. However, you need to invest time to learn these things. What I have witnessed is that some leaders give away movie tickets while most of the team either do not like to go to the movies or don't care for the film itself. It all depends on you to make it meaningful, specific, and personal; this is the secret!

Always create a motivating environment. Do your best to make people want to come to work; create a positive external environment—the hygiene part of the two-factor theory. Always find activities that make the team want to come to work; make them enjoy work. Even something as simple as changing the setup or decorations in the office can help; perhaps create monthly themes, such as "healthy food month." Try to do something; even if you don't control the office, you control the meetings, so do what you can to make work a happier place.

Let us talk about appreciation and recognition. Both are usually intangible, and they do not have to be accompanied by rewards. However, with rewards, there is always recognition because when you give someone a reward, it has to be for a reason. You give recognition for good behavior, one you desire in your teammates, because you want to reinforce that particular behavior. Where a reward is related to an achievement or something specific—for example, anniversaries—it has to be something that is solid. Appreciation, like rewards, can be ongoing, and less formal compared to recognition.

Recognition and appreciation, like rewards, need to be based on the individual's personal preference. I actually had one of my reporting managers telling me, "Please don't recognize me in public." Usually, recognition and appreciation presentations are done in public because others will see that you are serious about rewarding effort and would want to have the same recognition, so they will demonstrate the desired recognized behavior. Then you send a motivational message to your team. Then people will mimic that good behavior, and this is basically what you want.

Personally, I always liked recognition in public because it shows that my direct manager genuinely appreciates something I have done. I have always felt that I am competent. I like to engage in healthy competition with my colleagues and myself to bring value to the organization; in doing so, we push each other's skills and capabilities further. For me, public recognition works very well. Not so many of my direct managers had that in mind. Maybe they were thinking of giving me a raise or a promotion, when actually I would have been happy with meaningful personal recognition. I like promotions, but they do not happen every year! They're not number one on my list. That is why I recommend starting with small thank-you notes and public recognition today.

Make your acts of recognition and appreciation frequent and specific. Don't wait for six months to appreciate others. Always look for the positive side of things and recognize every improvement in your team. Even in meetings, just saying thank you is enough and is a good way to start and end the meeting.

Be specific about what you recognize and appreciate in a person and what behavior. Make it immediate; don't wait for a week to tell them that they did a good job. Be timely. Timing is crucial, especially as you don't have to buy anything for that person. Even if you want to buy something as a gift, seize the moment and tell them how you feel and how happy you are and how proud you are of them and their work; then you can always get the reward or the gift that you want to hand to that person later.

As I said earlier, involving team members is also an effective tool for motivating them.

I like to sum up how genuine, authentic motivation works with this line: "You can always inspire others by seeing greatness in them and help them see it as well."

LESSONS LEARNED

So, in this chapter we discussed the following:
- The difference between motivation and manipulation.
- How manipulation can negatively impact you, your personal brand, and legacy.
- How motivation is empowering and genuine.
- How to motivate ourselves and why.
- How to have the right motivated people on our side, as team members, to deliver exceptional results and reach our vision.
- How to treat individuals and team members as individuals, not as employees.
- How to celebrate our achievements.
- The right ways to give rewards and appreciate a recognized team member.
- What to reward and who to reward.

CALL FOR ACTION

Practice motivation. Take all that is mentioned in this chapter and develop your own motivation agenda, whether you are a team leader or team member. What is special about you as a leader? How will you be the number one motivator and the best one anybody has worked with or for? Keep that note and start practicing motivation today; make it personal, frequent, specific, and immediate. Make sure that you realize the difference between manipulation and motivation because motivation is not about your interests but those of the other person. Invest time with people so that they understand that you care about them enough to help them; assist them to see the greatness within themselves.

CONDITIONS FOR SUCCESS

Don't manipulate others in any single way, no matter what the circumstances. It is the worst thing that you can do; lying to the other person. It is not acceptable, and it means that you are not ready to pursue a valuable dream, a vision to become someone who will be considered a great role model for humanity. People, sooner or later, will know if you are manipulative or not; and once you have this stigma, you can never remove it or take what you have done from their memories. If you become famous, it will be even worse, as now you will be a famous manipulator.

If you have challenges in any of the items that we discussed in the motivation process, put it at the top of your to-do list and find ways to apply it in your leadership style.

Now we have covered the three main topics of the book on how to lead yourself, influence others positively and lead teams. In this chapter, we mainly covered motivation in depth—all you need to know and do to keep pushing yourself and others to achieve your vision. In the following chapter, we will sum up the overall learning in a direct and concise leadership model that I developed, the "Prevail Model," which includes the "Leadership Triangle."

SOURCES

https://www.discprofiles.com/blog/2018/09/teams-rewards-and-recognition/

Adrian Gostick and Chester Elton, 2009, The Carrot Principle

CHAPTER 6

THE PREVAIL LEADERSHIP MODEL

"Simplicity is the ultimate sophistication."

—Leonardo da Vinci

PREFACE

I n this chapter, we will end your learning journey in this book by combining the main ideas, tools, and skills of all four chapters of the book into what I call "The Prevail Leadership Model," which gives a clear model of how the four elements come together to help you achieve your vision, leave a memorable legacy and lead a joyful life.

This model will help you assess yourself and identify the areas that you need to focus on to balance your profile as per the Prevail Model in order to achieve the vision and desired results.

THE WHY AND THE WHAT

In a nutshell, if you want to be successful in your career, move to the next level, and leave a legacy that you can be proud of, the Prevail Leadership Model can be your starting point! It's the right development system to help you reach your goals!

Leaders often struggle to find a simple way to describe and validate their leadership practice. They have to decide what topics to cover and how to make the right connections in a visual, concise, and clear model for effective leadership. Leaders need to be focused, mindful, and resilient when addressing these challenges and leading their teams through good and bad times.

So, what can be a quick reference for leaders, one that will have a strong impact in both the short and long term? I have come up with the Prevail Leadership Model. This will be your reference to maximize your impact as an individual and as a leader. This Model contains the Leadership Triangle, which acts as the base for the Prevail Model.

The Leadership Triangle is divided into three elements: vision, competence, and change, with a supporting factor defined as fulfillment. Let me describe how all four elements come together.

The model is best described as a triangle: the top point is vision, the right point is competence, and the left point—and end result—is change. The leadership triangle can be applied as described below to any of the leadership situations: leading yourself, influencing others, and/or leading others.

As for the fulfillment factor, it is the fuel that keeps a leader moving forward toward their desired vision. It's the motivation that drives you to succeed in any situation.

THE HOW: HOW TO APPLY THE LEARNING IN A VISUAL, PRACTICAL, SIMPLE WAY!

THE LEADERSHIP TRIANGLE ™

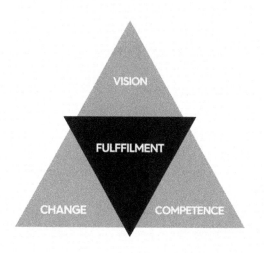

Here is an in-depth look at each part of the Leadership Triangle and how fulfillment contributes to them.

The vision part relates to personal vision, position, or strategy. Competence defines what capabilities you need to achieve the vision, while change is the end result. I thought a triangle would best represent the model as each element affects the other two. For example, we may define a personal vision that includes a demonstration of personal mastery, but we do not get the expected change; then either the vision is insufficiently defined or there is a problem with implementation. All three are interdependent. Fulfillment is measured by how excited and energized you are in achieving the vision. Below is a detailed description for each triangle.

SELF-LEADERSHIP TRIANGLE

Vision: personal vision based on values and passion.

Competence: personal mastery.

Change: define personal vision, personal life plan, live an intentional life.

Fulfillment: gratitude, well-being (Wheel of Life and enjoying life).

Evaluate yourself according to the "leading self" triangle by answering these questions: Do you know what you want in life? Do you know what you like to do, and can you do it well?

INFLUENCE TRIANGLE

Vision: dream, outcome, promise desired by self, and liked by others.

Competence: credibility and influencing skills.

Change: win others to your way (alliances, supporters, sponsors, and followers).

Fulfillment: helping others (mentoring, coaching, guidance, etc.).

"Am I there yet?" Are you considered a subject matter expert authority or trusted person/professional? Do you have a compelling dream, vision, or outcome?

Do you have followers and supporters? Do people trust you?

TEAM LEADERSHIP TRIANGLE

Vision: objective, goal, and team vision.

Competence: building teams and leadership skills.

Change: achieve exceptional results, make positive impact and experience, and exceed stakeholder expectations.

Fulfillment: motivate self and team members.

"Am I there yet?" Are you and your teams motivated? Do you create innovative and creative solutions? Are your team members highly engaged? Do they want to work with you?

In order to be a credible, influential leader who leads with impact and delivers exceptional results, all three leadership triangles must be fulfilled. This is a complex combination that gives any leader the tools to inspire others in achieving great things; it will put you on the right path toward building a remarkable legacy. You will prevail, no matter what challenges you face, because you will know how to optimize available resources and get the most out of any situation by relying on your support system while remaining authentic to your principles.

So the Prevail Model consists of leading self, influencing others, and leading teams through a fulfilling journey of authenticity, integrity, caring, and gratitude. The intention is not to reach your goal; the intention is to lead successfully while enjoying the journey!

THE PREVAIL LEADERSHIP MODEL^{TM}

SUMMARY OF MODEL

I have organized the main learning of the book in two parts: the Leadership Triangle and the Prevail Model.

The Leadership Triangle is divided into three parts: vision, competency, and change.

This Triangle applies to three leadership styles: leading self, influencing others, and leading others and teams.

Once all three leadership triangles are combined, they will present the Prevail Model. This is the ultimate model to help you lead in a genuine, authentic manner that makes you stand out from the rest.

Fulfillment is the fuel to keep you moving to achieve your goals in good health and with a positive mindset. It brings joy while you pursue your intentional life.

CONCLUSION

Your journey into this book has concluded the following takeaways:

- How to lead your life according to your values and acknowledge your strengths to stand out from the crowd.
- Why you need to influence others and how.
- How to get the right people on board in your team to build positive collaborative relationships by enhancing your communication and building your credibility.
- How to lead your team and stretch the team members' limits while keeping them motivated.
- Leadership Triangles that sum up the key elements of effective leadership, and are the core of the Prevail Model.
- The Prevail Model has the essentials of an impactful leader who others admire, look up to and, eventually, follow.

As you have gone through the book, it should have provided you with a clear idea of how successful leaders excel by being credible, authentic and influential.

You have learned how to master your leadership skills through helping others understand and attain their personal visions in their careers and lives, building strong relationships and reputations, supporting your objectives, and leading your team successfully.

By living an intentional, passionate life, doing what you like and doing it well, you will succeed in winning people over. If you do this while being a genuine and authentic leader, then you will be seen as an influential leader who delivers exceptional results and will be someone that others admire and trust. The Prevail Model can be your guide through times of self-doubt and confusion, helping you when you are in need of reassurance, while you achieve your personal vision and lead others in your own unique way. It has the recipe for success that will elevate both your inspirational life and career.

I will be happy to coach you through each of the Leadership Triangles, the Prevail Model and help you to develop general leadership skills. I can always be reached through LinkedIn at: abdulaziz-al-roomi, Twitter at: @abdulaziz_roomi, Facebook and Instagram at: abdulaziz.alroomi or email: ar@abdulazizalroomi.com.

For further information about the list of services provided, you can check my personal website: www.abdulazizalroomi.com.

Keep in mind that in order to benefit from the information and models, it's critical that you be honest and transparent with yourself at every step of the way, practice, do the required reflections and celebrate your achievements along the journey to keep yourself motivated.

As explained above, make sure the leading-self triangle is solid before you move to the next triangle.

Have a peer or an external coach act as an accountability partner while you are using the new skills.

Best of luck and Prevail!

WHISTLES OF ACKNOWLEDGMENT

I would like to thank my friend Dr. Saud Al-Thaqib, who recommended the idea of writing my own book.

I am also grateful to Soliman Arab and Mohamed Hosny from Vigor, who helped me find the right agency to publish my book.

My friend Ahmad Nagi for the awesome book cover and insights.

My thanks also go to Moustafa, Vanita and all the Passionpreneur team for their ongoing support!

Heartfelt gratitude to all those who were involved in my book-writing journey!

WRITER'S CREDENTIALS

1. A master's degree in Management and Business Administration with over sixteen years of experience in the fields of HR, training and leadership development.
2. Elite credentials in Learning & Development, the HR field, coaching, and over 3000 hours of experience in empowering and guiding leaders and high-potentials in their leadership journeys.
3. A Marshall Goldsmith Executive Leadership & Team Coach; Dale Carnegie Trainer; and other tops.
4. An HR leader, who has been exposed to and practiced best-in-class, world-class practices in leadership development and talent management.
5. Learned HR across industries, including retail, petrochemical, engineering, oil and gas, logistics, IT, food and beverage, banking and other sectors.
6. Experienced in developing leaders for the future through innovative training and development activities, coaching techniques and leadership assessment to meet global standards.
7. Identifies training needs for executives and senior professionals and devises quality assurance training programs and initiatives. He has supervised multimillion-dollar training budgets and exceeded the expectations of his clients.
8. Delivered and managed hundreds of successful training programs with an average success satisfaction rate of over 90%.

9. Has a proven record of positive behavioral development of leaders and teams and has his Sigma Green Belt for enhancing leader's positive behavior up to 30% within two years.
10. Was successfully able to change management practices to build effective employee engagement.

WRITER'S BIO

Abdulaziz holds a master's degree in Management and Business Administration and has over sixteen years of experience in the fields of HR, training, and leadership development, as well as elite credentials in Learning & Development, the HR field, and coaching. He has over 3000 hours of experience in empowering and guiding leaders and high-potentials in their leadership journeys. He is a Marshall Goldsmith Executive Leadership & Team Coach, a Dale Carnegie Trainer, and has other elite credentials.